# THIS BOOK
## BELONGS TO

..................................................................

..................................................................

# Author's Afterthoughts

With so many books out there to choose from, I want to thank you for choosing this one and taking precious time out of your life to buy and read my work. Readers like you are the reason I take such passion in creating these books.

It is with gratitude and humility that I express how honored I am to become a part of your life and I hope that you take the same pleasure in reading this book as I did in writing it.

Can I ask one small favour? I ask that you write an honest and open review on Amazon of what you thought of the book. This will help other readers make an informed choice on whether to buy this book.

**My sincerest thanks.**

# @COPYRIGHT 2024

The content contained within this book may not be reproduced, duplicated, or transmitted without direct written permission from the author or the publisher. Under no circumstances will any blame or legal responsibility be held against the publisher, or author, for any damages, reparation, or monetary loss due to the information contained within this book. Either directly or indirectly.

**Legal Notice:**

This book is copyright protected. This book is only for personal use. You cannot amend, distribute, sell, use, quote, or paraphrase any part, or the content within this book, without the consent of the author or publisher.

**Disclaimer Notice:**

Please note the information contained within this document is for educational and entertainment purposes only. All effort has been executed to present accurate, up-to-date, and reliable, complete information. No warranties of any kind are declared or implied. Readers acknowledge that the author is not engaging in the rendering of legal, financial, medical, or professional advice. The content within this book has been derived from various sources. Please consult a licensed professional before attempting any techniques outlined in this book. By reading this document, the reader agrees that under no circumstances is the author responsible for any losses, direct or indirect, which are incurred as a result of the use of the information contained within this document, including, but not limited to — errors, omissions, or inaccuracies.

# Table of Contents

| | |
|---|---|
| PART - A | 8 |
| NATURE AND IMPORTANCE OF MANAGEMENT | 9 |
| PRINCIPLES OF MANAGEMENT | 27 |
| BUSINESS ENVIRONMENT | 43 |
| PLANNING | 57 |
| ORGANISING | 71 |
| PART — B | 86 |
| FIXED AND WORKING CAPITAL OR FINANCIAL MANAGEMENT | 86 |
| SOURCES OF FINANCE | 100 |
| BANKING – LATEST TRENDS | 113 |
| MARKETING | 117 |
| SAMPLE PAPERS | 127 |

# CBSE

| Chapter in this book | Chapter Name | Page No. |
|---|---|---|
| | PART—A | |
| 1 | Nature and significance of management | 6-24 |
| 2. | Principles of management | 26-42 |
| 3. | Business environment | 44-58 |
| 4. | Planning | 60-74 |
| 5. | Organising | 76-91 |
| | PART—B | |
| 9. | Marketing | 129-139 |
| | Sample papers CBSE only 1 & 2 | 141-163 |

# ISCE/ISC (Commerce)

| Chapter in this book | Chapter Name | Page No. |
|---|---|---|
| | PART—A | |
| 1 | Nature and significance of management | 6-24 |
| 2. | Principles of management | 26-42 |
| 3. | Business environment | 44-58 |
| 4. | Planning | 60-74 |
| | PART—B | |
| 6. | Fixed and Working Capital | 94-109 |
| 7. | Sources of finance for Joint Stock Company | 110-124 |
| 8. | Banking --- Latest Trends | 125-127 |
| | Sample Papers 1 to 3 ISC/ICSE only | 164-189 |

# PSEB/ SIMILAR BOARDS

| Chapter | Chapter Name | Page | Marking |
|---|---|---|---|

| r in this book | | No. | Scheme |
|---|---|---|---|
| | PART—A | | |
| 1 | Nature and significance of management | 6-24 | 6 |
| 2. | Principles of management | 26-42 | 6 |
| 3. | Business environment | 44-58 | 4 |
| 4. | Planning | 60-74 | 7 |
| 5. | Organising | 76-91 | 7 |
| | PART—B | | |
| 9. | Marketing | 129-139 | 10 |
| | SAMPLE PAPERS PSEB ONLY | 190-208 | 40-40 |

# PART- A

# NATURE AND IMPORTANCE OF MANAGEMENT

(For All boards)

## M.C.Q – I (Detail explanation)

1. Management is
    a) Art of getting things done through others.
    b) Group activity that coordinates the efforts of different people in the organization.
    c) Not a single person that consummates the whole process of management.
    d) All of the above.

Management is the art of getting things done through others. It is not a single person activity but an activity of group of people that coordinates their efforts to achieve organizational goals.
Answer: (d) All of above

2. Anything – management is
    a) Zero
    b) Success
    c) Failure
    d) Both a and c

Anything minus management is nothing/zero/failure. There is no chance of success of organization without management.
Answer: (D) Both a and c

3. Management is nature of
    a) Simple Science
    b) Pure science
    c) Inexact science
    d) Perfect science

Management is a nature of science but it is not a pure science or an applied science. It is an inexact science because as its principles are subject to change with time, situations and human nature.
Answer: - (C) Inexact science.

4. Who is the father of modern management?
    a) Henry Fayol

b) F.W Taylor
c) Peter F. Drucker
d) Harold Koontz

> Henry Fayol is the father of classical management and F.W Taylor is the father of functional management. Hence Peter F. Drucker is called as the father of Modern management.
> Answer: - (c) Peter F. Drucker.

5. Management is multi-dimensional because
    a) Management of work, people and HRM
    b) Management of work and people
    c) Management of work and operations
    d) Management of work, people and operations.

> Management is the Multi-Dimensional process because it includes management of work, management of people and management by operations.
> Answer: - (d) Management of work, people and operations.

6. How many objectives does management have?
    a) 2
    b) 3
    c) 4
    d) 5

> Management have 3 main objectives: -
> - Organizational objectives
> - Social objectives
> - Individual objective
>
> Answer: - (b) 3

7. Which of following is not an organizational objective of organization:
    a) Profit earning
    b) Innovation
    c) Better quality goods
    d) Market improvement

> Management have some main organizational objectives: -
> - Growth

- Survival
- Profit earning
- Market improvement

Note: - Better quality goods are the social objective of organization Hence
Answer: - (c) Better quality Goods.

8. Provide better working conditions in the organization is the
    a) Individual objective of organization
    b) Social objective
    c) Organizational Objective
    d) Both a and c

Better working conditions for work is the main individual objective of management.
Answer: - (a) Individual objective

9. Anything – Management = Zero is showing the
    a) Importance of management
    b) Limitations of management
    c) Objectives of management
    d) Scope of management

Management is the important part of every organization to achieve their goals. Hence
Answer: - Importance of management.

10. Which is not the importance of management: -
    a) Achieving organizational goals
    b) Balance between efficiency and effectiveness
    c) Development of society
    d) Control environment pollution

To control the environment pollution is the main social objective of organization and not an importance of organization. Hence
Answer: - (d) Control environmental pollution

11. Efficiency means
    a) Complete the task.
    b) Complete the task within time
    c) Complete the task with minimum cost.
    d) Complete the task in time and minimum cost.

Efficiency means complete the whole task within time and with minimum cost.

Answer: (d)

12. Effectiveness is related to
    a) Process
    b) End result
    c) Activity
    d) Cost benefits

Effectiveness means complete the task within time only not matter what the cost is. It is just focus on the end result. Hence:
Answer: - (b) End result

13. What is the meaning of "doing things right" in the management?
    a) Doing the job in cost effective manner
    b) Doing the job, no matter whatever is the cost
    c) Doing the job only.
    d) Completer the job with all resources.

Doing the right things means doing the job, no matter whatever the cost. Doing things right means doing the job in cost effective manner.
Answer: - (a)

14. Management is to be poor if it is:
    a) Efficient but ineffective
    b) Effective but inefficient
    c) Both inefficient and ineffective
    d) All of above

Management become poor only when it will be both ineffective and efficient.
Answer: - (c)

15. Management not called as perfect science because
    a) Not related to human beings
    b) Related to human beings
    c) Related to art
    d) Related to experiments

Management is not called as perfect science because is related to human beings.
Answer: - (b)

16. Which is the responsibility of top-level management?
    a) Ensuring quality of output

b) Taking business responsibility for all activities and its impact on society
c) Ensuring the safety standards maintain in the organization
d) Assigning necessary duties to respective departments

> Top-Level Management is the level that contains the persons working at highest level of the organization like CEO, Directors, President, Chairman etc. Their main functions include the responsibility on whole organization i.e. important in whole organization. Hence quality of output in the hands of low level because they are closely related to workers and Society impact and necessary duties assign to departments in the hands of middle level management. Rest, Top-level must have to focus on Safety standards required in the organization. Hence
> Answer: - ©

17. Which of the following is the function of the middle-level management?
   a) Co-operate with other departments for smooth running of the organization.
   b) Responsible for welfare and survival of organization
   c) Interpreter the policies laid down by top-level management
   d) Responsible for all the activities done by operational departments

> Middle level management consists all the functional managers only i.e. purchase manager, sales manager, Production manager etc. So, it means their main function is welfare and survival of organization i.e. Top-level management not to corporate because its work of top-level mgt. Operational departments are not the part of middle level mgt, Hence, Not the answer of this question.
> Answer: - (b)

18. Which statement is not true for low-level management.
   a) Analyze the business environment and its implications
   b) Ensure for quality of output
   c) Strive to reduce the wastage of resources
   d) Ensure Best working condition in the organization

> Low-level management consists all the persons that directly supervise the work in the organization like inspectors, foreman, supervisors etc. So, Quality of output, its wastage and better conditions should be maintained are the responsibilities of this level. In short, Business environment and its impact on business must be seen by top-level management. Hence this is not true on part of low-level management
> Answer: - (a)

19. Identify which of following level of management not directly interact with work-force:

a) Operational management
b) First-line managers
c) Supervisory level
d) Middle-level management

Operational, first-line and Supervisory all the other name of low-level management and only low-level management are directly related to work-force. Hence
Answer: - (d)

20. How many main functions does management have?

a) 4
b) 5
c) 6
d) 8

Management have 5 main function as a process: - Planning, Organizing, Staffing, Directing and Controlling.
Answer: - (b)

21. Which of following is the primary function of management?

a) Planning
b) Organizing
c) Controlling
d) Coordination

Management have 5 main functions in a process namely
1. Planning
2. Organizing
3. Staffing
4. Directing
5. Controlling
Answer: - (a)

22. Functions of management defined as

a) PODSCORB
b) POSDCOR
c) PODSCOORB
d) POSDCORB

POSDCORB –
P- PLANNING
O- ORGANIZING

S- STAFFING
D- DIRECTING
CO- CONTROLLING
R- REPORTING
B- BUDGETING
Answer: - (d)

23. In POSDCORB, what does S stands for

   a) Supervision
   b) Supervising
   c) Staffing
   d) Shifting

S- stands for Staffing.
Answer: - ©

24. It is the force that binds all the functions of management

   a) Co-operation
   b) Coordination
   c) Planning
   d) Management hierarchy

Coordination means synchronization all the activities or functions of management.
Answer: - (b)

25. Coordination is

   a) Important part of every management
   b) Essence of management
   c) Process to bind all the activities of management
   d) All of above

Coordination is the process of binding all the activities of management. It is a main part of every management as well as considered as essence of every management.
Hence:
Answer: - (d)

26. The essence of management is

   a) Cooperation
   b) Coordination
   c) Directing
   d) Organization

Coordination is useful at every level of management and important with every function of management. Hence considered as the essence of management.
Answer: - (b)

27. Identify the process that provides requisite amount, timing, quality and sequence of efforts, which ensures that planned objectives are achieved with minimum of conflicts:
   a) Cooperation
   b) Coordination
   c) Planning
   d) Management

Coordination is the only process that helps in doing all the planned objectives with quality efforts and timing as well in sequence or with minimum conflicts.
Answer: - (b)

28. Coordination is considered as Essence of every management because.
   a) Important part of every management
   b) Needed at every level of management
   c) Important with every function of management
   d) All of above

Management is considered as essence every management because it is must in evert management, or at its every level as well as without it, no function of management possible. Hence,
Answer: - (d)

29. Which one is not the importance of management?
   a) Integrating various interest groups
   b) Developing society
   c) Disciplining employees
   d) Inculcating creativity

Management helps in integrate various interest groups as well in developing employees. But the main thing is discipling the employees in the organization regarding work is not the importance of management.
Answer: - (c)

30. At What level of management is coordination required?
   a) Top-Level management
   b) Middle-level management
   c) Operational-level management
   d) All three level of management

Coordination is the essence of management because not a separate function of management and important with every function of management as well as at every level of management. So,

Answer: - (d)

## M.C.Q – II (Case Study Based)

1. Suresh Sethi & Sons is well-known company that have main focus to synchronize their activities to achieve organizational goals effectively. Identify the main part of management discussed in the line.

   a) Controlling
   b) Coordination
   c) Planning
   d) Efficiency

Coordination is the synchronization or binding of various activities of the organization.

Answer: - (b)

2. Planning, Production, Purchase, Sales and Marketing departments are the main departments of XYZ manufacturing company. All the persons working in their departments cooperate with each other. But there is less harmony in the activities of these all departments which results in lack of positive results.

Identify the main problem that lacking here.

   a) Lack of efficiency
   b) Lack of planning
   c) Lack of effective control
   d) Lack of coordination

Answer: - (d) Lack of coordination

Hint to find Answer: - There is less harmony in the activities of the departments.

Note: - Students must remember the meaning of every concept during case studies.

3. Your uncle is working as "Marketing Manager" in a company. At what level of management is he working?

   a) Top-Level
   b) Middle-Level
   c) Operational level
   d) All levels

Answer: - Middle level management. (b)

> Hint to get answer: - Keep in mind all the functional managers are working at middle level management. So, Marketing manager is also a functional manager.

4. Your father was the retired director of the company. At what level he was working actually?

   a) Top-Level
   b) Middle-Level
   c) Low-Level
   d) All levels

> Answer: - (a) Top-Level
>
> Hint to find answer: - Students keep in mind that Director is the higher post in every company. Hence, Top-Level is the only level that includes all the persons working at higher positions in the organization like director.

5. Raman is working as "Plant Superintendents" in the Nifco Ltd. Name the managerial level at which he is working.

   a) Top-Level
   b) Middle-Level
   c) Low-Level
   d) Non-managerial level

> Answer: - (b) Middle level
>
> Hint: - Students please not to confuse it here that with the word Plant superintendents because he is also the functional manager in the organization that supervise the plant departments. So, its not lower-level, it is middle level management.

6. Raman, Suresh and Samar are the workers in the company Whoopers. They are connected with whole departments in the organization and also earns more profit for their company.

Choose the correct level at which Raman, Suresh and Samar working.

   a) Top-Level management
   b) Low-level management
   c) Platform area/ Non- managerial level
   d) Middle level management

> Answer: - (C)
>
> Hint: - Workers are come under non-managerial level. Student keep in mind that Actually there are four levels but at fourth level or platform area workers are working and that directly supervise by operational level or lower level of management.

7. There are 780 workers that actually works in the company. Superiors and Superintendents are also here to keep proper eye on them and on their work. They also pass their grievances to other level of management and then motivate them to work again with full efficiency and effectiveness to achieve goals.

About Which level of management discussed in above lines that pass worker grievances and motivate them also.

   a) Operational level management
   b) Non-managerial level
   c) Middle level management
   d) Top-Level management

Answer: - (a) Operational level management

Hint: - Superintendents and supervisors are the persons only working at low-level/ Operational level of management.

8. Reliance Pvt Ltd. is the well-known Company that cross their sales to 700 crores in just 10 months of the last year. Now they determine the objective to cross it by 1000 crores, so that they try to earns more profits and grow their business in the world market more and more.

The function of which level of management discussed above.

   a) Operational level management
   b) Middle level management
   c) Top level management
   d) Both Top and middle level management

Answer: - (C)

Hint: - Determine the objective is the main function of every Top-Level management.

9. MOMI TRADING CO. have just checked their grievances list and analyzed that their workers want to increase efficiency in work by improving some conditions. So as an objective company ask low level management and ensuring about proper ventilation, water, electricity and cleanliness etc.

Tell which of following function of low-level management discussed above.

   a) Submitting workers grievances in time.
   b) Ensure proper working conditions
   c) Ensure proper supply of every raw material
   d) Ensure the affect the environment.

Answer: - (b) Ensure Proper working conditions.

Hint: - Ventilation, Cleanliness, Electricity etc. are the main parts of working conditions.

10. Amisha as a Director of the Company, Whirlpool decides all important things i.e. What to do, how to do, when to do etc. to successfully perform the work. She also set various standards so that compared it with actual performance. She also direct, guide and instruct all the staffing workers just after planning without harmonious adjustments. As a result, Company sometimes faces lack of fixing their responsibility in best manner.

Which function Amisha and Co. actually lacking?

a) Planning
b) Cooperation
c) Organizing
d) Staffing

Answer: - (C)

Hint: - Organization means harmonious adjustments of work in different departments and it helps in fixing of responsibilities by relationship between authority and responsibility.

11. In planning process, XYZ Ltd Co. sets standards that the company will achieve the turnover of Rs1000 crores by March 2021. Management decide to achieve this goal efficiently and effectively. Suggest the all functions management need to perform after that set standard.

a) Planning, Staffing and controlling
b) Only Controlling
c) Planning, Organizing, Staffing, Directing and Controlling
d) Organizing, Staffing, Directing and Controlling.

Answer: - (d)

Hint: - Company decide the standards at planning process. So it is clear that planning step already done.

12. Ms. Bharti passed her M.B.B.S. examination in the first division in 2006. Later on, the year 2009 she passed her M.S. examination as an eye specialist. She was awarded a gold medal in this examination. After completing her studies, she joined a big hospital as an eye surgeon. She is performing ten operations successfully every year.

Now tell, What aspect of Ms. Bharti above experience is a science and what is Art?

a) Studying of eye specialist is science and gold award is art
b) Study of MBBS is science and MS are art
c) Study of MBBS and M.S. is science and working as eye surgeon is Art.
d) Study of eye surgeon is Both art and science.

Answer: - (C)

Studying M.B.B.S. and M.S. is science because get specialized knowledge and Working as eye surgeon is art because you are using his skills that you learn.

13. Mrs. Amisha Panwar passed her B. Sc. (Non-Medical) examination in the year 2006. After this she successfully ran the business of her father. Suddenly, she thought of seeking employment. She got the job of a finance manager in a company on the basis of her knowledge, experience and proficiency. She is doing her job successfully.

Now tell, Is the employment of Mrs. Amisha Panwar as a manager valid?

   a) Yes
   b) No
   c) May be
   d) Need to do MBA

Answer: - Yes (a)

14. Rahul wants to start his own departmental store and try to manage their finance, activities, efficiency and effectiveness in their work to achieve maximum profits. He wants to getting the things done by others with their group efforts. He wants actually the group of persons that run their departmental store with proper planning, and controlling.

Give the name of activity try to discuss above.

   a) Coordination
   b) Cooperation
   c) Organizing
   d) Management

Answer: - (d) Management

Hint: - Try to manage................
Planning and controlling
Group efforts etc. All shows that it is the management.

15. Hero LTD.'S target is to produce 20000 shirts per month at the cost of Rs150 per shirt. The Production manager could achieve this target at the cost or Rs 170 per shirt. Do you think the production manager is efficient?

   a) Yes, he is efficient
   b) No, he is not efficient
   c) May be due to slightly change in target
   d) None of above

Answer: - (b)

Hint: - Not efficient because he has achieved the target but not in cost-effective manner.

16. Volvo Ltd. target is to produce 10000 shirts per month at the cost 100 per shirt. The production manager achieved this target at cost 90 per shirt. Do you think the production manager is effective?

   a) Yes
   b) No
   c) Possible but 50-50
   d) None of above

Answer: - (a) Yes

Because he has to achieved the target.

17. ABC ltd. as a duty provide timely quality goods to the society.

Which objective of management shown above.

   a) Organization objective
   b) Social objective
   c) Personal Objective
   d) Both a and b

Answer: - (b)

Management have 3 main objectives. Social objectives are those that are based on society improvements.

18. Mega Ltd. manufactured water-heaters. In the 1$^{st}$ year of operations, the revenue of company was just sufficient to meet its costs. To increase the revenue, the company analyzed the reasons behind the less revenue. After analyzed company decided to reduce labour costs by shifting the manufacturing unit into backward area where labour was available at very low rates.

Identify the objective of management.

   a) Organizational
   b) Social
   c) Personal
   d) Both a and b

Answer: - Organizational

Hint: - Increase revenue for organization, labour was available at very less cost i.e. reduce costs.

19. Reliance Alliance Ltd. is a well-known cement company in India. The rate of profit of the company is very good. Company, as a result of it, always focus to satisfied their

employees with better working conditions so that they earn more and more for business and achieved their goals in best efficient manner.

Identify the objective of management discussed above

a) Social objective
b) Individual objective
c) Organizational objective
d) All of above

Answer: - (b)
Hint: - Better working condition is the individual objective of management.

20. XYZ Ltd. Co. is the well-known company is society. It always tries to achieve group goals. For that purpose, Company uses various resources i.e. Men, Material, Machine and money etc. in an optimum manner to increase the efficiency in the organization work and thereby reduce the cost.

Which importance of management is not highlighted in the above paragraph.

a) Helps to achieve group goals
b) Helps in optimum utilization of resources
c) Helps in reduction of cost
d) Helps in development of society

Answer: - Helps in development of society (d)

# M.C.Q – III (ASSERTION AND REASON)

ASSERTION(A): - Management is an art.

REASON(R): - It is the practical application of knowledge that requires personal skills.

Find the correct option: -

a) Both A and R are true and Reason is the correct explanation of Assertion.
b) Both A and R are true and R is not the correct explanation of A.
c) A is true and R is false.
d) A is false and R is true.

Management is an art of getting things done through others and also a practical knowledge of application that need practice and personal skills for doing work from others.

Answer: - (a) Both A and R are true and R is the correct explanation of A.

ASSERTION(A): - Management is a pure science.

REASON(R): - Management principles are subject to change with time, situations and human nature.

Find the correct option: -

a) Both A and R are true and Reason is the correct explanation of Assertion.
b) Both A and R are true and R is not the correct explanation of A.
c) A is true and R is false.
d) A is false and R is true.

> Management is not a perfect science because its principles are subject to change with time, situations and human nature.
>
> Answer: - (d) A is false and R is true.

ASSERTION(A): - Management is a group activity.

REASON(R): - It is rightly to said that nothing is eternal in management.

Find the correct option: -

a) Both A and R are true and Reason is the correct explanation of Assertion.
b) Both A and R are true and R is not the correct explanation of A.
c) A is true and R is false.
d) A is false and R is true.

> Management is a group activity because it is not done only by single person, it includes group efforts to achieve organizational goals.
>
> Yes, nothing is eternal in management, but not the reason for group activity. So,
>
> Answer: - (b) Both A and R are true and R is not correct explanation of A.

ASSERTION(A): - Management is the main part of every essential economic and social activities of the business.

REASON(R): - Anything – Management = Zero

Find the correct option: -

a) Both A and R are true and Reason is the correct explanation of Assertion.
b) Both A and R are true and R is not the correct explanation of A.
c) A is true and R is false.
d) A is false and R is true.

> Management is the main part of every organization because without it, it's difficult to

manage every business activity effectively and efficiently. So, anything if minus management then results to zero/failure/ Nothing.

Answer: - (a) Both A and R are true and R is the correct explanation of A.

ASSERTION(A): - Management is the process of work done by others in efficient and effective manner.

REASON(R): - The process of management includes all its functions such as planning, organizing, staffing, directing and controlling.

Find the correct option: -

a) Both A and R are true and Reason is the correct explanation of Assertion.
b) Both A and R are true and R is not the correct explanation of A.
c) A is true and R is false.
d) A is false and R is true.

Management is the planning, organizing, staffing, directing and controlling of work done in organization in effective and efficient manner.

Answer: - (a) Both A and R are true and R is the correct explanation of A.

ASSERTION(A): - Both managerial and non-managerial members are working in the organization.

REASON(R): - CEO, Directors, Departmental managers, supervisors as well as workers, all come under the category of managerial members.

Find the correct option: -

a) Both A and R are true and Reason is the correct explanation of Assertion.
b) Both A and R are true and R is not the correct explanation of A.
c) A is true and R is false.
d) A is false and R is true.

Yes, management has 2 categories: -

- Managerial
- Non-managerial

But workers are considered as non-managerial members and come under platform area of organization and all persons working at three levels of management are come under managerial members. So,

Answer: - (C) Assertion is True and Reason is False.

ASSERTION(A): - Middle level management creates link between top level management and lower level management.

REASON(R): - They passes instructions to lower level management given by top level and also get their grievances if any and then passes to top level for timely action.

Find the correct option: -

a) Both A and R are true and Reason is the correct explanation of Assertion.
b) Both A and R are true and R is not the correct explanation of A.
c) A is true and R is false.
d) A is false and R is true.

> Middle level management helps the both top and lower level management. It helps in creating link between two by passing the instructions to lower level persons and grievances to top level. Hence
> Answer: - (a) Both A and R are true and R is the correct explanation of A.

ASSERTION(A): - Coordination is important in every level of management as well as with every function of management.

REASON(R): - The essence of management is cooperation.

Find the correct option: -

a) Both A and R are true and Reason is the correct explanation of Assertion.
b) Both A and R are true and R is not the correct explanation of A.
c) A is true and R is false.
d) A is false and R is true.

> Coordination is the essence of management because it is not a separate function and has to perform with all other functions of management and at every level.
>
> Answer: - (c) A is true and R is False.

# PRINCIPLES OF MANAGEMENT

(For All Boards)

## M.C.Q – I (Detail explanation)

1. Management Principles are
    a) Basic truths that have ability to predict results of managerial activities.
    b) Guidelines that helps to solve the managerial problems.
    c) Guidelines for managerial decision-making and action.
    d) All of the above.

> The principles of management is the basic statement that provides understanding and guidance to thinking or action and solving the problems. It also predicts the better results for management.
> Answer: (d) All of above

2. Management principles are
    a) Contingent
    b) Static
    c) Definite
    d) Not directly concerned with human nature.

> Management principles are contingent because affected by lot of situations.
> Answer: (a) Contingent

3. Management principles are derived from
    a) Observations
    b) Experiments
    c) Both observations and experiments
    d) None of above.

> Management principles are derived on two bases: -
> - Observation
> - Experiments
>
> Answer: - (C) Both observation and experiments

4. Who is the father of Principles of management?
    e) Henry Fayol

f) F.W Taylor
   g) Peter F. Drucker
   h) Harold Koontz

> Henry Fayol is the father of classical management and also the Principles of management. F.W Taylor is the father of functional/Scientific management.
>
> Answer: - (a) Henry Fayol

5. Which of following principle helps in fixing the responsibility in the organization?
   a) Division of work
   b) Unity of direction
   c) Esprits de Crops
   d) Parity between Authority and Responsibility.

> According to principle of parity between authority and responsibility, Authority must go hand in hand. It must be balanced between authority and its responsibility. As a result, if responsibility defines easily then, its easy to fixing the responsibility.
>
> Answer: - (d) Parity between Authority and Responsibility.

6. Which of following principle of management affect the individuals only?
   a) Unity of direction
   b) Unity of Command
   c) Esprits de Crops
   d) Scalar Chain

> Unity of Direction, Esprits de crops and Scalar Chain, all affect the organization and Unity of command relates to individuals. Hence
>
> Answer: - (b) Unity of Command

7. The principle of Order implies:
   a) One head and One Plan
   b) Issuing instructions
   c) Settings things in order
   d) Proper direction to employees

> Principle of order states that a right person should be placed at right job and a right thing should be placed at right place.
>
> Answer: - (c) Settings the things in order.

8. Which of following principle of management relates to encourage team spirit?

a) Esprits de crops
b) Initiate
c) Stability of tenure
d) Equity

> Principle of esprits de crops states that a manager should make efforts to encourage the team spirit among all the workers so that group goals can be achieved easily.
> Answer: - (a) Esprit de crops.

9. What is the exception of scalar chain?

a) Emergency plan
b) Fayol's Ladder
c) Gang Plank
d) Direct route

> Scalar chain is the formal line of authority that flows from highest to lowest rank in straight line. But sometimes, due to emergency there is exception i.e. emergency route named Gang Plank.
> Answer: - (C) Gang Plank.

10. The principle that treats the employees in just and kind way.

a) Initiative
b) Equity
c) Fair Remuneration to workers
d) Esprits de crops

> Initiative is the principle that deals to give initiatives to employees for their best results.
> Equity related to equality in all workers i.e. Just and Kind for all.
> Remuneration to workers means timely fair wages given to workers
> Answer: - (b) Equity

11. One person receives order from one superior only. Which principle defines?

a) Unity of direction
b) Scalar Chain
c) Esprit de crops
d) Unity of command

> Unity of command is the principle that tells that one person receives order from only one superior.
> Answer: (d)

12. Who is the father of Functional management?

a) Henry Fayol
b) Peter F. Drucker
c) F.W. Taylor
d) Koontz O' Donnel

> F.W. TAYLOR – FUNCTIONAL / SCIENTIFIC MANAGEMENT
> HENRY FAYOL – CLASSICAL MANAGEMENT
> PETER F. DRUCKER – MODERN MANAGEMENT
> Answer: - (C) F.W. Taylor

13. Science not a Rule of Thumb is the
    a) Principle of Scientific Management
    b) Principle of Management
    c) Feature of Scientific management
    d) Fact.

> Science not a rule of thumb is one of the main principles of scientific management which means we should not stick only to one set routine with old machines, we continuously experiment to do something new.
> Answer: - (a)

14. Scientific management is useful only for: -
    a) Small organizations
    b) Large organizations
    c) Only production organizations
    d) Both small and large organizations

> Scientific management is useful only for the large organizations.
> Answer: - (b)

15. Which of following technique of F.W. Taylor helps in end up all conflicts between two parties.
    a) Functional Foremanship
    b) Motion study
    c) Differential peace wage rate
    d) Mental Revolution

> Mental revolution is the only technique that change the mind sets of workers and manager in the organization and it would be less chances of conflicts
> Answer: - (d)

16. Taylor suggested the division of work in two departments. What are two?

a) Production and Purchase departments
b) Production and planning departments
c) Production and Sales departments
d) Production and Marketing departments

Two departments namely production and planning departments are divided by F.W. Taylor in his technique functional foremanship. They marked these departments as two heads and then divided the specialists in these two.
Answer: - (b)

17. Putting an end to unnecessary types, sizes, qualities etc.
    a) Simplification
    b) Standardization
    c) Motion Study
    d) Functional Foremanship

Answer: - (A)

18. The rest during work is the part of
    a) Simplification of work
    b) Standardization of work
    c) Motion study
    d) Fatigue study

Fatigue study refers to determine duration and frequency of rest intervals to complete a particular job in time.
Answer: - (D)

19. Taylor Principles are applied
    a) In special situations
    b) Universally
    c) Factory areas
    d) None of above

Henry Fayol's Principles are applied everywhere i.e. universally but Taylor Principles are only applied in special situations

Answer: - (A) In special situations.

20. Movie camera is used in which of following study?
    a) Method Study
    b) Motion study
    c) Mental revolution

d) Time study

> Motion study refers to check the motions done by workers during work. This study try to eliminate unproductive movements and hence used movie camera to keep eye on them timely.
> Answer: - (b)

21. Main objective of method study is
    a) Minimize the costs
    b) Maximize the quality and level of consumer satisfaction
    c) Find out the alternate methods to do same work
    d) Both a and b

> Method study refers to study that identify the most suitable method to do a particular task from alternative ones. Its mainly wants to reduce costs and increase the consumer satisfaction
> Answer: - (D)

22. All the workers should work quickly: - ensure by
    a) Gang Boss
    b) Time and Card Clerk
    c) Speed Boss
    d) Inspector

> Speed boss should ensure that all the workers should work quickly or at required speed or expected speed.
> Answer: - (C)

23. Which of the following clerk decides the sequence of work?
    a) Instruction Card clerk
    b) Route Clerk
    c) Discipline officer
    d) Inspector

> Route clerk defines the sequence to do the tasks.
> Answer: - (b)

24. After preparing the instructions by instruction card clerk, he handover same card to
    a) Route clerk
    b) Time and cost clerk
    c) Gang Boss
    d) Inspector

Gang boss gets the cards of instructions and then starts the productions as a group leader and assign important responsibilities.
Answer: - (C)

25. Inspector comes under, (According to F.W. Taylor division)
    a) Planning departments
    b) Purchase department
    c) Production department
    d) Sales department

| Production departments includes: | Planning departments includes: |
|---|---|
| <ul><li>Gang Boss</li><li>Speed Boss</li><li>Repair Boss</li><li>Inspector</li></ul> Answer: - (C) | <ul><li>Route clerk</li><li>Instruction Card clerk</li><li>Time and cost clerk</li><li>Discipline officer</li></ul> |

26. Which principle of scientific management suggested that managers and workers jointly involve in every work and determine standards.
    a) Harmony Not Discord
    b) Cooperation not individualism
    c) Development of each and every person at his greater efficiency.
    d) None of above

Answer: - (b)

27. Fayol have how many principles?
    a) 10
    b) 12
    c) 14
    d) 16

Answer: - 14 (C)

28. The principle of unity of direction is related with
    a) Persons
    b) Activity
    c) Remuneration
    d) Profits

Unity of command is related to persons but unity of direction related to activity.

Answer: - (B)

29. Division of work results in
    a) Increases specialization
    b) Monotony
    c) Both a and b
    d) Effectiveness

Division of work results in increasing specialization as well as monotony. So
Answer: - (c)

30. Taylor Focus on
    a) Top-level
    b) Middle level
    c) Shop floor
    d) Lower level

Taylor mostly focus on the shop floor because its focus on working area i.e. on workers and they come under shop floor only.

Answer: - (C)

# M.C.Q – II (Case Study Based)

1. ABC Co. Ltd is the private limited company that is getting good profits in a year. In such a situation, Company continuously run their activities without giving any incentives to their workers. Due to lack of incentives or increase remuneration, many workers can leave the company. Now company facing new recruitment expenses and leads to loss instead of more profits for next year.

Which of the following principle of management is lacking here by ABC Co.?
    a) Principle of initiative
    b) Principle of remuneration to workers
    c) Principle of equity
    d) Principle of stability of tenure of personnel.

Hint: - After increasing profits, company not increases remuneration of their workers.
Answer: - (b)

2. A laborer completes 10 units of goods in a day. Another laborer who happens to be a relative or superior completes 8 unites per day. But both gets same remuneration. It means 2nd laborer gets less remuneration from 1st one.

Which principle of management lacking here?

a) Fair remuneration to workers
b) Equity
c) Initiative
d) Order

Answer: - (b) Equity

Hint to find Answer: - Both gets same remuneration instead of less output by 2nd laborer.

Note: - Students must remember the weather he is a relative of superior but management principles just follow on kind and equality.

3. A furniture manufacture gets an order for manufacturing 100 lecture stands. He has five workers to do the job. He efficiently distributes parts of lecture stands- legs, top board, center support, assembling and polishing to all five workers. This shows that he follows one of the main principles of Henry Fayol.

Now tell, which principle he follows here?

a) Unity of command
b) Scalar Chain
c) Division or work
d) Order

Answer: - (C) Division of work

Hint to get answer: - Keep in mind Division of work means divided the work into small tasks and then assign every small task to the worker who is specialized in its field.

4. Company ABC divides some decisions and authority in their subordinates. It divides that the decisions in respect of determination of objectives and policies, expansion of business etc. in hands of superior. On the other side, company also give authority to subordinates regarding some more short-term tasks like purchase of raw-material, granting leave to employees etc.

Now tell, which principle of management highlighted in above case?

a) Unity of command
b) Equity
c) Initiative
d) Centralization and Decentralization

Answer: - (D) Centralization and Decentralization

Hint to find answer: - Centralization means power in hands of one person i.e. superior. Decentralization means power in hands of many persons i.e. subordinates.

5. An employee working in a factory know about all the place from he gets tool in case of need. Similarly, he also knows the place where supervisor will be available in case of any need. Now tell, Which principle of management highlighted here.
   a) Centralization and Decentralization
   b) Scalar Chain
   c) Order
   d) Division of work

Answer: - (C) Order

Hint: - Principle of order states that right person should be placed at right jo

6. A purchase manager of company has to purchase 100 tons of raw material. His son happens to be supplier along with other suppliers in the market. The manager purchases raw material from the firm of his son at higher rate that the market. This will profit the manager personally but company will incur loss. This loss is undesirable.

Suggest the best principle that is important here.

   a) Principle of centralization and decentralization
   b) Principle of esprits de crops
   c) Principle of subordination of individual interest to general interest.
   d) Principle of initiative.

Answer: - (C)

Hint: - Manager showing his own individual interest not the business.

7. The production manager of Bharat Ltd. instructs a salesman to go slow in selling the product, whereas the marketing manager is insisting on fast to selling to achieve its targets. Which principle of management is being violated here?
   a) Unity of Direction
   b) Unity of command
   c) Order
   d) Authority and responsibility

Answer: - (B) Unity of command.

Hint: - unity of command means one subordinate should receive order from one superior only.

8. Mohan, the manager of business undertaking is very lax with his employees and subordinates. He does not give them parameters on rules for reporting to work and completion of assignments. Which principle of management is overlooked here?

   a) Equity
   b) Esprits de crops
   c) Unity of direction
   d) Discipline

   Answer: - (D)

   Hint: -Very lax with employees and not parameters given for any work showing its that it is principle of discipline.

9. Abhishek is the manager of company expects that his subordinates to adapt new environment and working conditions without giving them time to settle down. Which principle of management is being overlooked here.

   a) Scalar chain
   b) Initiative
   c) Stability of tenure
   d) Esprits de crops

   Answer: - (C) Stability of tenure

   Hint: - Because manager not giving so much opportunity to employees so that they settled.

10. CA Amisha Panwar adopting scientific management in her company. She likes one of the scientific techniques by F.W. Taylor to maintain Harmony between manager and workers of the company. Can you tell, which technique she likes?

    a) Differential peace wage rate system
    b) Functional foremanship
    c) Fatigue study and Motion study
    d) Mental revolution

    Answer: - (D)

    Hint: - Mental revolution is the technique that helps in maintaining the harmony between workers and managers and thereby conflicts will be end.

11. Aman is the Group leader that is selected as worker's group leader. He ensures that both the workers and machines are fit enough for production and the material be required for the use every time. Who is the leader?

    a) Speed boss
    b) Inspector

c) Repair boss
d) Gang boss

Answer: - (d)

Hint: -Gang boss is the group leader that ensure that all material as well as machines are fit enough for the use of workers.

12. CA Sachin Arora is the chartered accountant in the well-known Reliance company and audited that company is running very smoothly and finances are also managed easily by various sources of finance. But he noticed that sometimes the end use of production leads to create problem in the company regarding management of finance specially. He suggested them F.W Taylor technique for that purpose. What is that technique?

a) Standardization of work
b) Simplification of work
c) Method study
d) Functional foremanship

Answer: - (B)

Simplification or work refers to putting the end to unnecessary types, qualities, sizes, weights etc.

13. Suppose a company has standard output per day be 20units and the two-wage rate be Rs 5 and Rs 4 per unit respectively. Worker A produces 20 units in a day and in doing he earns Rs 100. Another worker B produces only 18 units in a day and hence earns only Rs 72. But with just 2 units less, difference in wage rates ranges to Rs28. So, Taylor suggested here to motivate inefficient workers to more work to cover and understand this difference.

Which of following technique highlighted here?

a) Esprits de crops
b) Fair remuneration to work
c) Initiate
d) Differential peace wage rate

Answer: - (d)

14. Company XYZ have aim to achieve group goals. Company, for that reason adapt the one of the principles of Henry Fayol to increase team spirit in their group. The relevance behind this principle is that the unity is relevant for all in this principle.

a) Order
b) Division of work
c) Discipline

d) Esprit de crops

Answer: - (d) Esprits de crops

Hint: - Esprit de crops refers that there must be team spirit and cooperation in management.

15. Santa Singh, a manager expects his subordinates to work for the happiness and pleasure of being in company. Point out the principle violated here.
    a) Order
    b) Initiative
    c) Remuneration
    d) Equity

Answer: - (C)

Hint: - Because manager try here his subordinates to get less remuneration or doing more to company.

# M.C.Q – III (ASSERTION AND REASON)

ASSERTION(A): - Management principles are the basic statements.

REASON(R): -It guide managers and workers to thought and action.

Find the correct option: -
    a) Both A and R are true and Reason is the correct explanation of Assertion.
    b) Both A and R are true and R is not the correct explanation of A.
    c) A is true and R is false.
    d) A is false and R is true.

Principle of management are basic statements that guide the managers and workers to action.
Answer: - (a) Both A and R are true and R is the correct explanation of A.

ASSERTION(A): - Management principles have cause and effect relationship.

REASON(R): -In division of work, whole work is divided into different parts and each part assign to person specialized in that field. As a result, specialization increases. Hence division of work is cause and specialization increases is the effect

Find the correct option: -
    a) Both A and R are true and Reason is the correct explanation of Assertion.

b) Both A and R are true and R is not the correct explanation of A.
   c) A is true and R is false.
   d) A is false and R is true.

> Answer: - (A) A is true and R is the correct explanation of A.

ASSERTION(A): - Management Principles are fixed in nature.

REASON(R): - They are affected by lot of situations.

Find the correct option: -

   a) Both A and R are true and Reason is the correct explanation of Assertion.
   b) Both A and R are true and R is not the correct explanation of A.
   c) A is true and R is false.
   d) A is false and R is true.

> Management principles are contingent because affected by lot of situations.
> Answer: - (D) A is false and R is True

ASSERTION(A): - There must be balance between authority and responsibility

REASON(R): - It results in lack of confidence among employees.

Find the correct option: -

   a) Both A and R are true and Reason is the correct explanation of Assertion.
   b) Both A and R are true and R is not the correct explanation of A.
   c) A is true and R is false.
   d) A is false and R is true.

> With the balance between authority and responsibility, employees get more confident and do more and more work.
> Answer: - (C).

ASSERTION(A): -There must be team spirit in the management persons according to esprit de corps.

REASON(R): - Esprit de corps is the main principle of management.

Find the correct option: -

   a) Both A and R are true and Reason is the correct explanation of Assertion.
   b) Both A and R are true and R is not the correct explanation of A.
   c) A is true and R is false.
   d) A is false and R is true.

> If advantage or disadvantage, any one of them written here in reason about team spirit

> then it is A otherwise it is B because R is true but not correct explanation.
> Answer: - (B)

ASSERTION(A): - Scientific management is the systematic approach to management and its use that all activities are completed in systematic manner.

REASON(R): -The father of scientific management is F.W. Taylor.

Find the correct option: -

a) Both A and R are true and Reason is the correct explanation of Assertion.
b) Both A and R are true and R is not the correct explanation of A.
c) A is true and R is false.
d) A is false and R is true.

> Both A and R are true. But R is not the correct explanation of A So, its
> Answer: - (B).

ASSERTION(A): - Science not a rule of thumb.

REASON(R): - We should not stuck in set routine with old techniques of doing work.

Find the correct option: -

a) Both A and R are true and Reason is the correct explanation of Assertion.
b) Both A and R are true and R is not the correct explanation of A.
c) A is true and R is false.
d) A is false and R is true.

> Answer: - (a) Both A and R are true and R is the correct explanation of A.

ASSERTION(A): - Motion study aims to increase the productive activity only without eliminating non-productive activities

REASON(R): - Motion study uses movie camera to check unproductive movements.

Find the correct option: -

a) Both A and R are true and Reason is the correct explanation of Assertion.
b) Both A and R are true and R is not the correct explanation of A.
c) A is true and R is false.
d) A is false and R is true.

> Motion study aims is to eliminate the unnecessary movements in the job.
> Answer: - (D) A is false and R is true.

ASSERTION(A): - In scientific management, a worker work under 8 specialists simultaneously

REASON(R): - Scientific management violates the principle of unity of command.

Find the correct option: -

a) Both A and R are true and Reason is the correct explanation of Assertion.
b) Both A and R are true and R is not the correct explanation of A.
c) A is true and R is false.
d) A is false and R is true.

Scientific management violates unity of command because a worker work under 8 specialists.
Answer: - (A)

# BUSINESS ENVIRONMENT

(For All Boards)

## M.C.Q – I (Detail explanation)

1. Business environment is the totality of
   a) External factors.
   b) Internal factors.
   c) Both a and b
   d) None of the above.

   Business environment is the sum total of all those factors that on which business have not control i.e. external factors
   Answer: (A) External factors

2. Which of following forces affected the industry separately?
   a) General forces
   b) Special forces
   c) Technical forces
   d) All of above

   Special forces are the forces that affect the industry separately such as customers, suppliers etc.
   Answer: (B) Special Forces

3. Social environment is the part of
   a) General forces
   b) Specific forces
   c) Dimensional forces
   d) All of above

   General forces are those that affect all the firms of industry equally such as social, economic, legal environment etc.

   Answer: - (A) General forces

4. Production methods are the main factor that affect
   a) Business environment
   b) Internal environment specially
   c) External environment
   d) Micro environment

   Production method is the internal factor that affect business environment and hence

come under internal environment.
Answer: - (B)

5. Which of following is not the part of micro environment?
   a) Public
   b) Market intermediaries
   c) Legal regulators
   d) Suppliers

Legal regulators are the part of macro environment because it has distant relation to business
Answer: - (C) Legal regulators

6. Which of following factor is closely related to business environment?
   a) Competitors
   b) Market intermediaries
   c) Economists
   d) Both a and b

Economists are come under economic environment and its macro factor that not closely relate to business. Hence both competitors and market intermediaries come under micro factor and closely part of business
Answer: - (D) Both a and b

7. Which is not a dimension of business environment?
   a) Social Environment
   b) Technological environment
   c) Demographical Environment
   d) Political environment

Answer: - (c) Demographical environment

8. Economic system not include
   a) Politic
   b) Socialistic
   c) Capitalistic
   d) Mixed economy

Economic system means the system that prevailing in our country. Mainly, three systems are here

- Socialistic

- Capitalistic
- Mixed economy

Answer: - (A) Politic

9. Under which system, business directly managed and control by government?
   a) Socialistic
   b) Capitalistic
   c) Mixed economy
   d) None of above

Capitalistic economic system is that in which business is control by private persons and socialistic include government only. So,
Answer: - (A) Socialistic

10. Mixed economy is prevailing which of following country?
    a) Canada
    b) U.S.A
    c) China
    d) India

India is the best example of mixed economy where both govt and individuals control businesses.
Answer: - (D) India

11. National income is an example of:
    a) Economic system
    b) Economic conditions
    c) Economic policies
    d) All of above

National income is the example of economic condition.
Answer: (B)

12. In the year 1977, the Janata Government adopted a stringent attitude towards the multidimensional companies like IBM and Coca Cola had ignore India.

The impact showing above is example of
   a) Political environment
   b) Natural environment
   c) Global environment
   d) Legal environment

> Political environment is the outcome of combinations of various ideology advocated by different political parties
> Answer: - (A) Political Environment

13. The examples of social factors are
    a) Customs
    b) Traditions
    c) Wishes
    d) All the above

> Answer: - (D)

14. With the increase in FDIs and Foreign Exchanges, many MNCs entered into Indian Market. Consequently, there has been tremendous increase in foreign exchange reserves in the country.
The impact of which environment shown in above example?
    a) Economic environment
    b) Legal environment
    c) Political environment
    d) Global environment

> It is legal environment because there are many acts like FEMA OR FERA were introduced to increase FDIs.
>
> Answer: - (b)

15. Which of following is not an economic reform?
    a) Liberalization
    b) Privatization
    c) Globalization
    d) Centralization

> Economic reforms are LPG. It means Liberalization, Privatization, and Globalization
> So, Answer: - (d)

16. Freeing the economy of country means
    a) Liberalization
    b) Globalization
    c) Privatization
    d) All the above

> Liberalization means freeing the economy from license system
> Answer: - (A)

17. When economic reforms were formed?
   a) 1990
   b) 1999
   c) 1991
   d) 1992

   Answer: - (C)

18. After globalization, FERA act was replaced by
   a) FESA
   b) FEMA
   c) FENA
   d) FERA 2

   FERA stands for foreign exchange regulation act and its replaced by FEMA which stands for Foreign exchange management act
   Answer: - (B)

19. Integrate the economy of country with rest of world is called.
   a) Liberalization
   b) Globalization
   c) Privatization
   d) Decentralization

   Globalization refers to integrate the country's economy with rest of world.
   Answer: - (B)

20. Nothing can be said with any amount of certainty about factors of business environment. Why?
   a) Because of totality of only external factors
   b) Because business environment is static
   c) Because business environment is changing quickly
   d) Because business environment is permanent in nature.

   Business environment is changing quickly. Hence it is difficult to get certain about its factors.
   Answer: - (C)

21. Name the policy that is framed to develop industries.
   a) Industrial policy
   b) Industrial license policy
   c) Industrial Act
   d) Foreign trade policy

> Industrial policy is the policy that was framed to develop industrial sectors
> Answer: - (A)

22. GST is covered under
    a) Economic reforms
    b) Social reforms
    c) Political reforms
    d) Legal reforms

> GST is the part of economy. Hence, include in economic reforms.
> Answer: - (A)

23. The development of science and technology depend on
    a) Public support
    b) Political stability
    c) Climatic conditions
    d) Literacy level

> Literacy level decides the development of science and technology.
> Answer: - (D)

24. The role of public sector reduce under which of following policy?
    a) Industrial policy 1991
    b) Liberalization
    c) Globalization
    d) Economic reforms

> Industrial policy 1991 reduce the public sector.
> Answer: - (A)

25. Which of following statement is correct?
    a) Liberalization refers to integrate the country's economy to whole world economy.
    b) Globalization refers to freeing the economy from license system
    c) Privatization means conversion of public sectors into private sectors.
    d) Public sectors reduce to just 1.

> Liberalization means freeing the economy from license system and Globalization means integrate the country's economy to rest of world economy.
>
> Public sector reduces to just 2 now not 1
>
> So, correct is

Answer: - (C)

# M.C.Q – II (Case Study Based)

1. Avantika and Abhishek both are good friends. But one day both get confused about business environment. Abhishek says it is the totality of both internal as well as external forces. But Avantika says it is totality of only external forces. Now solve their confusion or clashes about correct answer by choosing one from following.
   a) Avantika is right because both factors affect in business
   b) Abhishek is right because the nature of external forces also in totality and its uncontrollable
   c) Both are correct because it is difficult to explain environment
   d) Both are wrong as business environment not affected by any forces.

Abhishek is correct because only external forces are uncontrollable and its nature also totality. Hence best reason is 2.
Answer: - (b)

2. Government of India is seriously thinking to allow oil marketing public sector undertakings to fix their own price for petrol and diesel. Which economic reform is the reason of this change in government policy.
   a) Liberalization
   b) Privatization
   c) Globalization
   d) All the above

Answer: - (A)

Hint to find Answer: - Govt. try to REMOVE license from one industry and tells to fix own price. So, in short answer Globalization is not possible. But there is not privatization so simple it's also not a privatization.

3. Just after declaration of Lok Sabha Elections 2009 results, the Bombay stock exchange's price index (Sensex) rose by 2100 points in a day. Identify the environment factor affect lead to rise.
   a) Legal environment
   b) Political environment
   c) Economic environment
   d) Both a and b

Answer: - (B) Economy of politics

Hint to get answer: -LOK SABHA is the best example of politics.

4. Government of India announced in 1991 that all public undertaking must be converted into private sector, to make the country more advanced. It will help in reducing the fiscal burden of the government. Tell, about which reforms and government announced it
   a) Liberalization in economic reforms
   b) Privatization in economic reforms
   c) Globalization in political reforms
   d) Privatization in political reforms

Answer: - (B)

Hint to find answer: -Privatization means converting the public sectors into private sectors to make country more advanced.

5. Mohan and Govind after finishing graduation decided to start their own travel agency which book Air and Rail tickets on commission basis. They both concerned and analyze the business environment of the business they will going to start. They analyze the all social, economic factors as well as technological factors that affect the business directly and indirectly. They concerned more to improve technology and makes online best platform for all customers. It results in benefits to their business also.

Identify the component of business environment highlighted in above paragraph.
   a) Social environment
   b) Technological environment
   c) Economic environment
   d) Political environment

Answer: - (B)

Hint: - Improve technology and online platform.

6. Post demonetization in a further push to cashless economy, the central Cabinet has recently approved the ordinance for paying wages via electronic, means. Accordingly, the govt. approved to Amend section 6 of payment of wages act 1936, to allow employers of certain industries to make payments through the electronic modes and cheques. The new ordinance will be applicable to public sector.

Identify various dimensions of business environment discuss in above paragraph.
   a) Political and legal
   b) Political, legal and technological
   c) Technological, economic and legal
   d) Legal, political and economic

Answer: - (B)

Hint: - Govt. approved showing political & Act comes under legal and electronic means technological.

7. As a result of the decision by Britain to exit to European Union the new trade agreements will come into force from EU as it accounts for 35-40% of auto components exports from India. Tata Motors owned Britain's largest carmaker Jaguar Land Rover has been in Britain for three decades and makes 475000 cars a year in country of which most of them are exported inside EU and beyond. JLR estimates that their annual profit could be cut by one billion pounds by the year 2020

Name the components of business environment discusses above.

   a) Economic and legal
   b) Legal and social
   c) Legal and political
   d) Political and economic

Answer: - (C).

Hint: - Britain means Britain govt. So, its political and agreements shows legal environment also.

8. The government wants to raise Rs 567500 crore from sale of stake in state owned enterprise National Thermal Power Plant (NTPC) in the financial year 2016-2017.

   a) Privatization
   b) Liberalization
   c) Disinvestment
   d) Investment

Answer: - (C)

Hint: - Disinvestment means transfer in public enterprise to private sector through dilution of stake of government in public enterprise

9. With changes in the consumption habits of people, Neelesh, who was running a sweet shop, shifted to the chocolate business. On the eve of Diwali, he offered chocolates in attractive packages at reasonable prices. He anticipated huge demand and created a website chocolove.com for taking orders online. He got a lot of orders online and earned huge profits by selling the chocolate.
Identify the dimensions of business environment discussed in the above case.

   a) Social and technological
   b) Social only

c) Technological only
d) Economic, Social and technological.

Answer: - (A)

Hint: - Consumption habits is a main factor of social environment.
Chocolove.com (online) is the example of technological environment.

10. A recent rate cut in the interest on loans announced by the banks encouraged Amit, a science student of Progressive School, to take a loan from State Bank of India to experiment and develop cars to be powered by fuel produced from garbage. He developed such a car and exhibited it in the Science Fair organized by the Directorate of Education. He was awarded the first prize for his invention. Identify the dimensions of business environment discussed in the above case.

a) Economic environment only
b) Political environment only
c) Both political and economic environment
d) Economic and technological environment.

Answer: - (D)

Hint: - rate cut on interest loans by banks – Economic
Developed cars or science exhibition show – Technological

11. After independence, Govt. of India saw that economy of country gone to decline and in very difficult situation. There was a need to cut off the country from economic difficulty and speeding up the growth. As a result, Govt announced various economic reforms in 1991 with new economic policy. Which was the main common reforms?

a) Liberalization and privatization
b) Liberalization and globalization
c) Privatization and globalization
d) Liberalization, Privatization and Globalization

Answer: - (D)

12. There is a firm that only supplies goods to the government and earns lot of earnings sometimes in case of huge orders. But after that the closure of that firm have large chances than others because in case govt. stops buying from that market then supply stops. There will be no earnings and business closed.

Now tell, only one customer affects the firm. What type of factor is it that is uncontrollable?

a) Macro factor
b) Micro factor
c) Internal factor

d) Both a and b

Answer: - (B)

Customers are the micro factors and come under external environment and uncontrollable or less controllable.

13. The ASIAN PAINTS a leading company of paint industry, at one stage lagged behind because of technology. This was smartly understood by another company, GOODLASS NEROLAC (GN). In order to exploit this situation, the latter company entered into the contract with foreign company named KANSAI PAINTS (KP) with the purpose of acquiring the latest technology The KP made available to GN the Cathodic Electro Deposition (CED) technology. On the very basis, the GN was able to obtain the contract for entire paint requirement of the MARUTI UDYOG. In this way GN earned huge profits by entering into market with latest technology.

Now tell which of following advantage of business environment is highlighted above.

a) Tapping useful resources
b) Coping with Rapid changes
c) Assist the best Planning and get benefits for long run
d) First mover advantage.

Answer: - (D)

GN company enter in market and point out weakness of Asian paints and then after new technology establishment, company gets MARUTI UDYOG contract for paints. Hence First move to get advantage.

# M.C.Q – III (ASSERTION AND REASON)

ASSERTION(A): - Business environment is the totality of all external factors

REASON(R): - As business environment is a group of many outside forces. That's why its nature is totality.

Find the correct option: -

a) Both A and R are true and Reason is the correct explanation of Assertion.
b) Both A and R are true and R is not the correct explanation of A.
c) A is true and R is false.
d) A is false and R is true.

Business environment is the totality of all external factors because the nature of all outside group also is of totality.

Answer: - (a) Both A and R are true and R is the correct explanation of A.

ASSERTION(A): - It is difficult to control on business environment.

REASON(R): - Only internal environment is controllable.

Find the correct option: -

a) Both A and R are true and Reason is the correct explanation of Assertion.
b) Both A and R are true and R is not the correct explanation of A.
c) A is true and R is false.
d) A is false and R is true.

> R is true but not correct explain A because there is need of more reasons why difficult?
>
> Answer: - (B) A is true and R is NOT the correct explanation of A.

ASSERTION(A): - Business environment happens to be different in different countries.

REASON(R): - There is no relativity in the business environment.

Find the correct option: -

a) Both A and R are true and Reason is the correct explanation of Assertion.
b) Both A and R are true and R is not the correct explanation of A.
c) A is true and R is false.
d) A is false and R is true.

> Business environment is relative in nature. Hence different in different countries.
> Answer: - (C) A is TRUE and R is FALSE

ASSERTION(A): - Business environment is certain in nature.

REASON(R): - It going to change quickly.

Find the correct option: -

a) Both A and R are true and Reason is the correct explanation of Assertion.
b) Both A and R are true and R is not the correct explanation of A.
c) A is true and R is false.
d) A is false and R is true.

> Business environment is uncertain but yes! Continue to change quickly.
> Answer: - (D).

ASSERTION(A): - Competitors, suppliers and customers directly affect the business than other environments.

REASON(R): - Other environment includes economic environment, social environment, political etc.

Find the correct option: -

a) Both A and R are true and Reason is the correct explanation of Assertion.

b) Both A and R are true and R is not the correct explanation of A.
c) A is true and R is false.
d) A is false and R is true.

R is not fully correct to A BECAUSE R should be that it is due to micro environment that directly related to business.

Answer: - (B)

ASSERTION(A): -There are three economic systems in India.

REASON(R): - India have Capitalistic economy.

Find the correct option: -

a) Both A and R are true and Reason is the correct explanation of Assertion.
b) Both A and R are true and R is not the correct explanation of A.
c) A is true and R is false.
d) A is false and R is true.

India have MIXED ECONOMY. SO,
Answer: - (C).

ASSERTION(A): - The country is now freeing from any license system.

REASON(R): - It is due to liberalization.

Find the correct option: -

a) Both A and R are true and Reason is the correct explanation of Assertion.
b) Both A and R are true and R is not the correct explanation of A.
c) A is true and R is false.
d) A is false and R is true.

Answer: - (a) Both A and R are true and R is the correct explanation of A.

ASSERTION(A): - New economic was announced in year 1999.

REASON(R): - New economic policy is the policy that was announced by govt. of India to speeding up the industrial growth in the country.

Find the correct option: -

a) Both A and R are true and Reason is the correct explanation of Assertion.
b) Both A and R are true and R is not the correct explanation of A.
c) A is true and R is false.
d) A is false and R is true.

New economic policy was announced in year of 1991.

Answer: - (D) A is false and R is true.

ASSERTION(A): - SWOT analysis means the analysis of company's strength, weakness, Opportunities and Threats.

REASON(R): - SWOT can be modified as TOWS.

Find the correct option: -

a) Both A and R are true and Reason is the correct explanation of Assertion.
b) Both A and R are true and R is not the correct explanation of A.
c) A is true and R is false.
d) A is false and R is true.

BOTH A and R are true But R is not full correct explanation of A.

Answer: - (B)

# PLANNING
(For all boards)

## M.C.Q – I (Detail explanation)

1. Planning is the
    a) 1st function of management
    b) 2nd Function of management
    c) 3rd function of management
    d) Last function of management

   Answer: (A) First Function

2. Which of following statement is right?
    a) If you fail to plan, you will be failed.
    b) Your plan decides the path.
    c) If you plan to fail, define the right path.
    d) If you fail to plan, you plan to fail.

   Answer: (D)

3. The manager who acts without planning must learn to live without
    a) Profit
    b) Earnings
    c) Survival
    d) failure

   Answer: - (A) Profit

4. Planning is
    a) Thinking in advance
    b) Thinking in future
    c) Thinking continuously
    d) Thinking effectively

   Planning is thinking in advance what to do, when to do, how to do, why to do and by whom is to be done?
   Answer: - (A)

5. Which of following statement is false?
    a) Planning focuses on achieving objectives

b) Planning is pervasive
c) Planning and forecasting are same
d) Planning is intellectual process.

> Planning and forecasting are not same.
> Planning is the term given to the process of coming up with plans for the upcoming future. It is based on the past and present performance of the company. On the other hand, Forecasting is the term given to the process of making predictions about a future event.
> Answer: - (C)

6. Planning is mental exercise because
    a) It is futuristic
    b) It helps the business to think easily
    c) It helps manager to decide what to do, when to do etc.
    d) It is continuous process.

> Planning helps manager in deciding what to do, when to do, how to do, why to do and by whom to be done? Hence helps to intellect or mental exercise
>
> Answer: - (C)

7. Planning is needed at
    a) Top-level
    b) Middle level
    c) Lower level
    d) All levels

> Planning is pervasive in nature. Hence needed at all levels of management.
> Answer: - (D) All levels

8. Planning does not work in
    a) Static environment
    b) Dynamic environment
    c) Mixed environment
    d) Business environment

> Planning does not work under dynamic environment. Future is uncertain and hence planning based on future not always works.
> Answer: - (B)

9. The first step of planning process is

a) Setting objectives
   b) Developing premises
   c) Identifying best course of action
   d) None of above

> Planning process always starts by setting the objective.
> Answer: - (A)

10. After identifying the alternate course of action, the next step in planning process is
    a) Select an alternative
    b) Evaluate an alternative
    c) Developing premises
    d) Implement the plan

> After developing premises, alternative course should identify and then must evaluate so that it will be selected.
> In short - Answer: - (B) Evaluate the alternative.

11. Raw material is a part of
    a) Internal premises
    b) External premises
    c) Both internal and external
    d) None of above

> Raw material is the internal assumption/premises.
> Answer: (A)

12. Planning is process and plan is its
    a) Starting
    b) Part
    c) Ending
    d) Outcome

> Planning is the process and plan is its outcome.
> Answer: - (D) Outcome

13. Every organization has central goal which is also called
    a) Objective
    b) Mission
    c) Policy
    d) Strategies

> Answer: - (B)

14. Objectives are
    a) End points for attainment of which all the activities are undertaken.
    b) Unambiguous
    c) Measurable
    d) All of above.

Answer: - (D)

15. The plans that are prepared to cope up from the competitors
    a) Objectives
    b) Strategies
    c) Policies
    d) Budget

Answer: - (b)

16. The plans that refers to determine the sequence of any work performance.
    a) Procedure
    b) Policies
    c) Methods
    d) Programmes

Answer: - (A)

17. The plan that refers to those general statements which to bed decided for guidance of employees while decisions.
    a) Policy
    b) Procedure
    c) Programmes
    d) Rule

Answer: - (A)

18. A single use plan laying down the what, when, why and how of accomplishing the specific job.
    a) Rules
    b) Procedure
    c) Programmes
    d) Methods

Answer: - (C)

19. Which of following plan describe the results in numerical form?

a) Policy
b) Procedure
c) Programmes
d) Budget

Answer: - (d)

20. Which plan define "What is to be done and what is not to be done?"
    a) Method
    b) Rule
    c) Budget
    d) Objectives

Answer: - (b)

21. A budget is related to
    a) Both planning and controlling
    b) Only planning
    c) Only controlling
    d) Planning, controlling and coordination

Answer: - (a)
Budget refers to plan that describe the desired results in numerical terms and related to both planning and controlling because controlling and planning are related to each other.

22. "No smoking in factory." It is an example of
    a) Objective
    b) Policy
    c) Programmes
    d) Rule

Rule define what is to be done and what not be done. So, no smoking in factory defines the rule
Answer: - (d)

23. To reduce the quality rejects to 3% is the example of which of following plan?
    a) Rule
    b) Methods
    c) Objective
    d) Policy

Objectives tells what is to be achieved. So, reduce quality shows 3% reduce the quality. Answer: - (C)

Note: - If questions ask about how then it must be policy as an answer.

24. Which is not true about planning?
    a) Planning reduce creativity
    b) Planning creates rigidity
    c) Planning works in dynamic environment
    d) Planning does not guarantee success.

Answer: - (C) BECAUSE Planning not works in dynamic environment.

25. Planning is continuous process because
    a) Plan prepared for particular period and hence need to be made new one after expiry.
    b) In case of any discrepancy in plan, it must revise
    c) In case of rapid changes, plan also need to revise.
    d) All the above.

Answer: - (D)

# M.C.Q – II (Case Study Based)

1. A Company decides to achieve annual sales of Rs 12 crore. After deciding upon this objective, planning to achieve objective shall immediately come into force. It was thought to achieve this objective by giving advertisements in the newspapers. After sometime it come to be known that the medium of advertisement appeared to be incapable of achieving the target. In such a situation the medium of advertisement can be changed and can be shifted from newspaper to television. In this way, every possible change is made through the action for the purpose of achieving goals.

Which of following feature highlighted in above para.
    a) Planning sets objectives
    b) Planning focuses to achieving objectives.
    c) Planning helps to set objectives
    d) Planning involve in decision making

Planning focuses on achieving goals.
Hint: - medium shifted or every possible change to focus on same objective to be achieved.
Answer: - (b)

2. XERO decides to expand their business and give authority to top level. Rest to sell the products or the decisions regarding this authorize to middle and lower level.

Which of the following planning features highlighted above two?

   a) Planning is important everywhere
   b) Planning is pervasive in nature
   c) Planning brings decisions making
   d) Planning helps to mental exercise.

> Answer: - (B) Pervasive
>
> Hint to find Answer: - DECIDES/PLAN by every level.
>
> Note: - Students must remember the meaning of every concept during case studies.

3. A Company is planning to market a new product. While doing so it shall have to keep in mind the taste and preferences of people and also the possibility of any change in them.

Which of following planning features highlighted above.

   a) Planning is Mental exercise
   b) Planning involve choice
   c) Planning is futuristic.
   d) Planning bring efficiency

> Answer: - (C)
>
> Hint to get answer: - Keep in mind all the tastes and preference + changes about future.

4. XYZ Co. fixed a sales target under planning. Now all the departments e.g. planning, sales, production, finance etc. will decide their objectives in view to achieve sales target. In this way, the attention of all the managers will get focused on attainment of goals. This will make achievement of goals efficiently. Thus, in absence of objective, an organization get disabled and objectives laid down under planning.

Which of following importance of planning above. (100% accurate)

   a) Planning sets objectives
   b) Planning provide direction.
   c) Planning brings decision making
   d) Planning promote innovative ideas.

> Answer: - Direction (B)
>
> Hint to find answer: - Sets objective not here because, planning sets + achieve objective. And above para also highlighted the achievement. But it gives direction. So, 100% is direction.

5. A new govt brings up new trade policy, policy of taxation, import policy etc. All these changes make every sort of planning a meaningless waste. Similarly, a change in policies of competitors suddenly make all type of planning ineffective.

Which of following factor highlighted above?

   a) Internal inflexibility
   b) External inflexibility
   c) Both a and b
   d) None of above.

Answer: - (b) External inflexibility.

Hint: - political change is the external factor.

6. A company wants to expand its business. It has an alternative to establish a factory in rural area. In this case company assume to be capital, raw material and labour as in business, and used industry policy for external factor. The manager looks out all the factors and assumptions so to make the planning process effective.

Which of following step of process of planning highlighted above.

   a) Setting objective
   b) Identifying the best alternative
   c) Evaluate the best alternative
   d) Developing premises

Answer: - (D)

Hint: - Labour, capital etc. ate internal premises and industrial policy is external premises/assumption

7. Star Ltd. company have two alternatives. But during planning process, it finds out that one alternative can be highly profitable only with high investments and also have long gestation period to yield profits. On the other hand, another alternative needs less capital investment with short gestation period but not have sufficient profits. So, company planner than again evolves new alternative course by mixture of different alternative course.

Which step of planning process actually done by company in above para?

   a) Identifying the alternative course of action
   b) Evaluating alternate course
   c) Selecting an alternative
   d) Implement of plan.

Answer: - (B)

Hint: - Company already have alternative so identifying not here.

> There is not a proper selection of alternative because company check out from available so its just a evaluation.

8. Super Fine Rice Ltd. has the largest share of 55% in the market. The company's policy is to sell only for cash. In 2015, for the first-time company's number one position in the industry has been threatened because other companies started selling rice on credit* also. But the managers of Super Fine Rice Ltd. continued to rely on its previously tried and tested successful plans which didn't work because the environment is not static. This led to decline in sales of Super Fine Rice Ltd. The above situation is indicating two limitations of planning which led to decline in its sales.

   a) Does not guarantee success and huge costs
   b) Huge cost and time consuming
   c) Does not guarantee success and not work in dynamic environment
   d) Not work in dynamic environment and rigidity.

> Answer: - (C)
>
> Hint: - successful plans don't work – guarantee success and environment is not static – not work in dynamic.

9. Shalini, a home science graduate from a reputed college, has recently done a cookery course. She wished to start her own venture with a goal to provide 'health food' at reasonable prices. She discussed her idea with her teacher (mentor) who encouraged her. After analyzing various options for starting her business venture, they short listed the option to sell readymade and 'ready to make' vegetable shakes and sattu milk shakes. Then, they weighed the pros and cons of both the shortlisted options.

Name the function of management highlighted above.

   a) Controlling
   b) Coordination
   c) Planning
   d) Staffing

> Answer: - (C) PLANNING

10. Rahul, a worker, is given a target of assembling two computers per day. Due to his habit of doing things differently, an idea struck him which would not only reduce the assembling time of computers but would also reduce the cost of production of the computers. Instead of appreciating him, Rahul's supervisor ordered him to complete the work as per the methods and techniques decided earlier as nothing could be changed at that stage. The above paragraph describes one of the limitations of the planning function of management. Name it.

a) Reduce creativity
b) Increases costs & time
c) Not guarantee success
d) None of above

Answer: - (A)

Hint: - Due to his habit of doing things differently, an idea struck him

11. The term demonetization has become a household name since the government pulled the old Rs. 500 and Rs. 1,000 notes out of circulation in November 2016. Prior to the year 2016, the Indian government had demonetized bank notes on two prior occasions—once in the year 1946 and then again in the year 1978. In both cases, the purpose was to combat tax evasion by 'black money'. Identify the types of one of the functions of management being discussed in the above lines.

a) Objectives
b) Strategy
c) Both a and b
d) Objective, strategy and method

Answer: - (C)

Hint: -. Prior to the year 2016, the Indian government had demonetized bank notes on two prior occasions—once in the year 1946 and then again in the year 1978. (STRATEGY)

In both cases, the purpose was to combat tax evasion by 'black money'. (OBJECTIVE)

12. Apna Ghar/ a company dealing in consumer durables, plans to increase the sale of its products by 25% around Diwali this year. Moreover, in order to cash on the implementation of the seventh pay commission by that time, which is likely to raise the income of 47 lakh serving employees of the Central government and 52 lakh pensioners, the company has created 30 advertisement films which will be aired across 85 national and regional channels until Diwali.
Now tell, which plans highlighted in above para?

a) Objectives and strategy
b) Objective and policies
c) Objectives and methods
d) Strategy and methods

Answer: - (A)

Objective: "Apna Ghar', a company dealing in consumer durables, plans to increase the sale of its products by 25% around Diwali this year."

Strategy: "Moreover, in order to cash on the implementation of the seventh pay commission by that time which is likely to raise the income of 47 lakh serving employees of the Central government and 52 lakh pensioners, the company has created 30 advertisement films which will be aired across 85 national and regional channels until Diwali."

## M.C.Q – III (ASSERTION AND REASON)

ASSERTION(A): - Planning is the thinking after doing.

REASON(R): - It helps in deciding what to do, when to do, why to do, how to do etc.?.

Find the correct option: -
a) Both A and R are true and Reason is the correct explanation of Assertion. \
b) Both A and R are true and R is not the correct explanation of A.
c) A is true and R is false.
d) A is false and R is true.

Planning is thinking before doing and helps in deciding what to do, when to do, how to do and when to do etc.
Answer: - (D) A is false and R is True.

ASSERTION(A): - Planning is the primary function of management.

REASON(R): - All other functions follow planning. Without planning, its not possible to perform.

Find the correct option: -
a) Both A and R are true and Reason is the correct explanation of Assertion. \
b) Both A and R are true and R is not the correct explanation of A.
c) A is true and R is false.
d) A is false and R is true.

Planning is the 1st function of management because all others function performs after planning, otherwise not possible.
Answer: - (A) A and R true and R is the correct explanation of A.

ASSERTION(A): - Planning is pervasive in nature.

REASON(R): - It is performed and needed at every level of management.

Find the correct option: -
a) Both A and R are true and Reason is the correct explanation of Assertion. \

b) Both A and R are true and R is not the correct explanation of A.
c) A is true and R is false.
d) A is false and R is true.

> Planning is important to be needed at every level of management. Hence, pervasive in nature.
>
> Answer: - (A) Both A and R are true and R is correct explanation of A.

ASSERTION(A): - Planning is an intellectual process.

REASON(R): - It is thinking about what to do only.

Find the correct option: -

a) Both A and R are true and Reason is the correct explanation of Assertion. \
b) Both A and R are true and R is not the correct explanation of A.
c) A is true and R is false.
d) A is false and R is true.

> R is totally wrong because planning is thinking in advance what to do, when o do, how to do, why to do etc.
>
> Answer: - (C) A is true but R is False.

ASSERTION(A): - Planning is a continuous process.

REASON(R): - The manager done the planning function at every level and before doing anything to perform.

Find the correct option: -

a) Both A and R are true and Reason is the correct explanation of Assertion. \
b) Both A and R are true and R is not the correct explanation of A.
c) A is true and R is false.
d) A is false and R is true.

> Planning is continuous process because it is prepared for particular period and there is need to make new plan after that.
>
> Answer: - (B) Both A and R are true but R is not correct explanation of A.

ASSERTION(A): - Planning works in dynamic environment.

REASON(R): -Planning is based on anticipations of future happenings.

Find the correct option: -

a) Both A and R are true and Reason is the correct explanation of Assertion. \
b) Both A and R are true and R is not the correct explanation of A.

c) A is true and R is false.
d) A is false and R is true.

> Planning is not work under dynamic environment.
> Answer: - (D) Assertion is False and Reason is True.

ASSERTION(A): - The planning process starts with setting objectives.

REASON(R): - After setting objectives, it needs to identifying alternative for plan.

Find the correct option: -

a) Both A and R are true and Reason is the correct explanation of Assertion.
b) Both A and R are true and R is not the correct explanation of A.
c) A is true and R is false.
d) A is false and R is true.

> After setting objectives, premises will be developed and then alternative identified.
> Answer: - (C).

ASSERTION(A): - THE EXAMPLE OF RULE IS - DON'T USE MOBILE PHONES DURING OFFICE WORKING HOURS.

REASON(R): - It is a rule that defines us what is to be done and what not to be.

Find the correct option: -

a) Both A and R are true and Reason is the correct explanation of Assertion.
b) Both A and R are true and R is not the correct explanation of A.
c) A is true and R is false.
d) A is false and R is true.

> Answer: - (A).

ASSERTION(A): - Recover the money from debtors in written letter is the example of procedure.

REASON(R): - Procedure is the method to done the task

Find the correct option: -

a) Both A and R are true and Reason is the correct explanation of Assertion. \
b) Both A and R are true and R is not the correct explanation of A.
c) A is true and R is false.
d) A is false and R is true.

> Procedure means plan to determine the sequence of any work performance.

Answer: - (C).

ASSERTION(A): -Planning is futuristic.

REASON(R): -It decides the plan of action- what to be done, when to be done, how to be done etc. all are the questions to future.

Find the correct option: -
a) Both A and R are true and Reason is the correct explanation of Assertion.
b) Both A and R are true and R is not the correct explanation of A.
c) A is true and R is false.
d) A is false and R is true.

Planning is futuristic because it decides the plan to action in future by deciding about various question like what to done, when to done, why to done etc.

Answer: - (A).

# ORGANISING

(For CBSE/PSEB and Some other several boards)
Not for ICSE/ISC in Term-1

## M.C.Q – I (Detail explanation)

1. Organising is the
    a) First function of management
    b) Second function of management
    c) Third function of management
    d) Fourth function of management

Answer: (B) First Function

2. Which of following statement is true about organising?
    a) Organising is the structural framework within which various efforts are coordinated and related to each other.
    b) Organising makes the administration ineffective.
    c) Organising is the 2nd function of management that follows staffing.
    d) Organising helps in supervision of employees works.

Answer: (A).
Organising is the second management function that helps in making the administration effective and follows planning to make the structural framework where efforts are coordinated

3. Organising include
    a) Group of persons
    b) Specialization
    c) Coordination
    d) All the above

Answer: - (D)

4. Organising involves
    a) Group goals
    b) Departmental goals
    c) Common goal
    d) Individual goals

Organising involves group of persons that working together in the organization to

achieve common objective.
Answer: - (C)

5. Organization is the
   a) Machine of management
   b) Heart of management
   c) Backbone of management
   d) All of above

Organization called as machine of management.
Heart of management is directing.

Answer: - (A)

6. Which of following is not the importance of organising?
   a) Proper use of all resources
   b) Effective administration
   c) Monotony
   d) Aid to management.

Monotony is the limitation of organising.
Answer: - (C)

7. Organising is importance for management same as
   a) Liver in human body
   b) Backbone in human body
   c) Heart in human body
   d) Structure of bones in human body

Organising is very much important in management as same as structure of bones in human body.
Answer: - (D)

8. The first step in the process of organising is
   a) Grouping jobs
   b) Division of work
   c) Assign duties
   d) Delegation of authority.

Organising is the process of division of work – grouping jobs – assign duties – delegate authority and last coordinate activities.
Answer: - (B)

9. There are two types of organizations. (100% valid)
   a) Divisional and Functional organization
   b) Formal and informal organization
   c) Line and staff organization
   d) All the above.

> Two types are mainly formal and informal.
> Functional and divisional are the structures of organization.
> Line and staff called as separate one.
> Answer: - (B)

10. The organized and official structure with clearly defined authority and responsibility relationship is called
    a) Line organization
    b) Informal organization
    c) Formal organization
    d) Divisional organization

> Formal organization is the official structure that formally and clearly defined the activities and fixed the responsibilities in the organization.
>
> In short - Answer: - (C) Formal Organization.

11. Which of following organization not based on any rule and regulation?
    a) Formal organization
    b) Informal organization
    c) Both a and b
    d) None of above

> Formal organization involves all rules and regulations but informal not.
> Answer: (B)

12. Which is not a true for formal organization?
    a) It creates stability in organization.
    b) It causes delay in work.
    c) It has independent channel of communications.
    d) It is based on division of work.

> Independent Channels are the part of informal organization.
> So, Answer: - (C)

13. Which of following statement is not true for informal organization?
    a) It is stable.

b) It is not deliberately created.
c) It is personal
d) It is not based on rules and regulations.

Answer: - (A) – stability is the feature of formal organization.

14. The organization refers to natural grouping of people in work situation to meet personal needs called
    a) Informal organization
    b) Formal organization
    c) Line organization
    d) Staff organization

Answer: - (A)

15. Which organization refers to direct chain of command through which authorty flows from top to bottom?
    a) Staff organization
    b) Line organization
    c) Formal organization
    d) Informal organization.

Answer: - (B)

16. If line organization connects with staff organization to makes the organization line and staff, then structure or nature or new organization would be?
    a) Simple
    b) Complex
    c) Both simple and complex in different situations.
    d) None of above.

Answer: - (B)

17. The division of whole organization according their activities they performed, then it is called?
    a) Line organization
    b) Staff organization
    c) Functional organization
    d) Divisional organization

If divide according to products manufactured then it is divisional, but now it is

Answer: - (c)

18. In which of following organization, there is chances of duplication of jobs?

   a) Line organization
   b) Functional organization
   c) Divisional organization
   d) All the above

> The cost of divisional structure is high only because of duplication of jobs.
> Answer: - (C)

19. What is not true about functional organization?

   a) It is based on work.
   b) It is specialized in products.
   c) It has no high costs.
   d) There is no duplication in functional organization.

> Products refers to divisional structure so it shows that functional organization is not specialized in products, it is specialized in jobs or work.
> Answer: - (B)

20. Divisional organization is useful when

   a) There are all types of firms
   b) There are diversified firms
   c) There are industrial firms
   d) Thera are monopoly firms

> DIVISIONAL IS BASED ON DIVERSIFIED.
> Answer: - (b)

21. Difficulty in inter departmental coordination – is the one of the limitations of which of following organization?

   a) Divisional organization
   b) Functional organization
   c) Both a and b
   d) Line organization

> Answer: - (B)
> FUNCTIONAL ORGANZIATION FEELS DIFFICULT TO DIVIDED TO ORGANIZATION ON BASIS OF PRODUCTS OR CREATE INTER DEPARTMENTS COORDINATION.

22. The number of employees on whom supervisor can successfully put his control is called?

a) Organising
b) Delegation
c) Span of control
d) Administration

> Span of control refers to number of employees on whom supervisor can successfully put his control. It is the concept only come under this function of management.
>
> Answer: - (C)

23. Assigning the work to others with giving full authority is called?

a) Authority
b) Delegation of authority
c) Decentralization
d) Organising

> Delegation refers to assigning the work to others and giving them some authority to do it.
> Answer: - (B)

24. Which is not the element of delegation of authority?

a) Authority
b) Responsibility
c) Accountability
d) Delegation

Answer: - (D).

25. Authority moves from

a) Top to bottom
b) Bottom to top
c) Right to left
d) Can't delegated

> Answer: - (A)
> Authority is the power to take decision given by superior to his subordinates.

26. Responsibility flows from

a) Top to bottom
b) Bottom to top
c) Can't flows
d) Both a and b

> When authority gives, responsibility automatically attached to that so it doesn't mean to

be top to bottom. But it means you have responsibility to complete the work. So,

Answer: - (B) Bottom to top

27. Accountability can be delegated to
    a) Top to bottom
    b) Bottom to top
    c) Both a and b
    d) Can't delegated

Accountability can't delegate because it means answer to the responsibility that given to you.

Answer: - (d) Can't Delegated

28. The essence of responsibility is
    a) To be dutiful
    b) To be owner
    c) To be efficient
    d) To be responsible

Responsibility involves the duty to do task.
Answer: - (A) TO BE DUTIFUL

29. Which of following is the basis for delegation of authority?
    a) Accountability
    b) Responsibility
    c) Organising
    d) Division of work

Authority comes into force only with division of work. Hence called as basis for it
Answer: - (D)

30. What is decentralization?
    a) Powers in the hand of only one person
    b) Powers in the hands of many persons
    c) Power in the hands of company's heads
    d) Power in the hands of HRM.

Decentralization refers to powers in the hand of many persons i.e. all levels.

Answer: - (B)

31. Decentralization includes
    a) Less freedom
    b) More freedom
    c) No freedom
    d) None of above

> More freedom because power in hands of many persons.
> Answer: - (B)

32. Deal in the business of many products instead of single one, is called
    a) Decentralization
    b) Delegation
    c) Diversification
    d) Expansion

> Answer: - (C)

# M.C.Q – II (Case Study Based)

1. XEROX Co. Ltd has business of large scale. Mr. Sachin Arora is the CEO of this company. He directs the sales manager that can take decisions to spend up to RS 1 Lakh in order to improve the performance of his division. It will help the company to earn more and increasing efficiency in work.

Choose from following about the exact concept discussed above?
    a) Decentralization
    b) Delegation
    c) Organising
    d) All the above

> Its delegation because –
> Direct sales manager only to take decisions.
> Answer: - (b)

2. There are two departments in the organization. One is A and other is B. Both departments have their own separate levels i.e. Top, middle and lower level. Department A decides that only top level get decisions for any work performing in department while department B wants to connect the subordinates and hence give power to all levels to decide about running of department in smooth way.

Choose from below the two main concepts discuss above followed by dept. A and dept. B?

a) A- Delegation & B- Decentralization
b) A – Decentralization & B – Delegation
c) A – Delegation & B – organising
d) A & B both organising

Answer: - (A)
Hint to find Answer: -
A – ONLY TOP LEVEL
B – ALL LEVELS

3. Mr. Suresh is the Chief Manager of the company. He gives authority to every departmental head to appoint employees in their departments. They further delegated their authority to deputy managers to reduce work burden. Mr. Suresh as a chief manager feels very relaxed and happy with the work of his company.

Which concept is highlighted above?

a) Decentralization
b) Delegation
c) Expansion of decentralization
d) Both a and c

Answer: - (D)

Hint to get answer: - He gives authority to every departmental head to appoint employees in their departments. (Decentralization)

They further delegated their authority to deputy managers to reduce work burden (Expansion of decentralization)

4. XYX Co. Ltd is the largest manufacturing company in the country. A company decides about dividing the work into many small parts and then want to starts the process by assigning responsibility to reduce work load in company. After assigning duties, company CEO, decided to granting authority for successful work performance. At last, CEO also try to hold the subordinates accountable for their work.

Now identify, which process is highlighted in above para?

a) Organising
b) Delegation
c) Decentralization
d) Organization

Answer: - Direction (B)

Hint to find answer: - Process of delegation involves

- Assigning responsibilities
- Granting authority
- Fixing responsibility.

5. Aman Ltd. is manufacturing toys and has production, sales, purchase and finance departments. Which type of organizational structure would you suggest to them?
   a) Functional organization
   b) Divisional organization
   c) Informal organization
   d) Line organization

Answer: - (A) Functional.

Hint: -because most suitable for such type of companies. .

6. Surekha runs a shoe manufacturing factory. She wants to expand her business. For expansion she contemplates to enter into manufacturing of leather bags and western formal wear apart from the running business of shoes. By doing this her company will be able to provide many products to working women under one roof.

Which organizational structure will you suggest here?
   a) Functional
   b) Line and staff
   c) Divisional
   d) Both a and c

Answer: - (C)

Hint: - BECAUSE IT GIVES EQUAL IMPORTANCE TO ALL PRODUCTS.

7. ABC organization is the organization that is directed by group norms. Which type of organization is it?
   a) Formal organization
   b) Informal organization
   c) Functional organization
   d) Line and staff organization

Answer: - (B)
Hint: - Group norms created only in informal groups.

8. The management of Hero ltd. company decides to plan the various objectives to be achieved for future. It also fills their all vacancies in organization and then direct them how to work. The objectives can be achieved or standards that set during planning can be achieved only by comparison of actual performance. But here the problem arises that management skip the mechanism of management. So, it results in planning to be worst.

Tell, what is the mechanism of management?

   a) Delegation
   b) Coordination
   c) Organising
   d) Division of work.

Answer: - (C)

Hint: -Skip second function of mgt, called as mechanism of management.

9. Kiran Industries is a company dealing in office furniture. The company chose to diversify its operations to improve its growth potential and increase market share. As the project was important, many alternatives were generated for the purpose and were thoroughly discussed amongst the members of the organization. After evaluating the various alternatives, Sukhvinder, the Managing Director of the company, decided that they should add 'Home Interiors and Furnishings' as a new line of business activity.

Name the framework, which the diversified organization should adopt, to enable it to cope with the emerging complexity?

   a) Functional
   b) Divisional
   c) Line and staff
   d) Formal

Answer: - (B)

It leads to faster decision making, promotes flexibility and initiative because each division functions as an autonomous unit.

10. Alliance Ltd. is engaged in manufacturing plastic buckets. The objective of the company is to manufacture 100 buckets a day. To achieve this, the efforts of all departments are coordinated and interlinked and authority-responsibility relationship is established among various job positions. There is clarity on who is to report to whom. Name the function of management discussed above

   a) Coordination
   b) Controlling
   c) Planning
   d) Organising

Answer: - (D)

Hint: - To achieve this, the efforts of all departments are coordinated and interlinked and authority-responsibility relationship is established among various job positions. There is clarity on who is to report to whom.

# M.C.Q – III (ASSERTION AND REASON)

ASSERTION(A): - Division of work is the basis for organization. Organization divides the whole work into many small tasks.

REASON(R): - It brings specialization and increase efficiency in work.

Find the correct option: -

a) Both A and R are true and Reason is the correct explanation of Assertion.
b) Both A and R are true and R is not the correct explanation of A.
c) A is true and R is false.
d) A is false and R is true.

Organization divides the whole work into small parts to brings specialization and efficiency in every task.

Answer: - (A) Both A and R are true and R is the correct explanation of A.

ASSERTION(A): - Organising makes the communication effective.

REASON(R): - As it specifies that who report to whom?

Find the correct option: -

a) Both A and R are true and Reason is the correct explanation of Assertion.
b) Both A and R are true and R is not the correct explanation of A.
c) A is true and R is false.
d) A is false and R is true.

Organising specifies clearly that who report to whom? In this way it clarifies the authority and responsibility relationship. So, communication also become effective.

Answer: - (A) A and R true and R is the correct explanation of A.

ASSERTION(A): -Organising is the process in which group of persons working together for achievement of common goals.

REASON(R): - The process of organising is firstly division of work, then to built departments, after that assigning duties and last to clarify authority and responsibility relationship.

Find the correct option: -
   a) Both A and R are true and Reason is the correct explanation of Assertion.
   b) Both A and R are true and R is not the correct explanation of A.
   c) A is true and R is false.
   d) A is false and R is true.

> Yes, it's true by both sides that organising is group activity for achievement of common goals and process is also correct but reason should define why common goals not process. Hence, not correct explanation of A.
> Answer: - (b) Both A and R are true and R is not correct explanation of A.

ASSERTION(A): -Formal organization is more stable.

REASON(R): - It changes its structure with very much needs and tastes of individuals.

Find the correct option: -
   a) Both A and R are true and Reason is the correct explanation of Assertion.
   b) Both A and R are true and R is not the correct explanation of A.
   c) A is true and R is false.
   d) A is false and R is true.

> Stable because of not changes with tastes and needs of individual.
> Answer: - (C) A is true but R is False.

ASSERTION(A): - Informal organising is deliberately created.

REASON(R): - It emerges out of mutual relationships and tastes.

Find the correct option: -
   a) Both A and R are true and Reason is the correct explanation of Assertion.
   b) Both A and R are true and R is not the correct explanation of A.
   c) A is true and R is false.
   d) A is false and R is true.

> Yes, it emerges from mutual relations but not deliberately created. So,
> Answer: - (D) A IS FALSE AND R IS TRUE.

ASSERTION(A): -Functional organization easily established coordination.

REASON(R): -All persons working in it are specialists in their respective jobs.

Find the correct option: -
  a) Both A and R are true and Reason is the correct explanation of Assertion.
  b) Both A and R are true and R is not the correct explanation of A.
  c) A is true and R is false.
  d) A is false and R is true.

> R is exactly correct one reason for A.
> Answer: - (A) Both A and R true and R is correct explanation of A.

ASSERTION(A): - Divisional organization results in duplication of jobs.

REASON(R): - Divisional organization formed on the basis or products.

Find the correct option: -
  a) Both A and R are true and Reason is the correct explanation of Assertion.
  b) Both A and R are true and R is not the correct explanation of A.
  c) A is true and R is false.
  d) A is false and R is true.

> Both are correct but here the R is not properly correct explanation because R must be for the duplication of jobs i.e. R will be that its due to costs.
>
> Answer: - (B).

ASSERTION(A): - All authority, responsibilities and accountability are the elements of delegation.

REASON(R): - All elements can be delegated.

Find the correct option: -
  a) Both A and R are true and Reason is the correct explanation of Assertion.
  b) Both A and R are true and R is not the correct explanation of A.
  c) A is true and R is false.
  d) A is false and R is true.

> Accountability cannot delegate.
> Answer: - (C). A TRUE BUT R FALSE

ASSERTION(A): - Decentralization results in slow decision making.

REASON(R): - In decentralization, power in hands of many persons.

Find the correct option: -
  a) Both A and R are true and Reason is the correct explanation of Assertion.

b) Both A and R are true and R is not the correct explanation of A.
c) A is true and R is false.
d) A is false and R is true.

> Many persons mean quick decision making. Hence here R true but A false.
> Answer: - (D)

ASSERTION(A): -There is limited chance of development in functional organization.

REASON(R): - It is versatile in nature.

Find the correct option: -

a) Both A and R are true and Reason is the correct explanation of Assertion.
b) Both A and R are true and R is not the correct explanation of A.
c) A is true and R is false.
d) A is false and R is true.

> Due to specialize only in one kind of job, there is limited chances of development. So, A is true but R is false
> Answer: - (C).

# PART—B

# FIXED AND WORKING CAPITAL OR FINANCIAL MANAGEMENT

(Special for ISC AND ICSE)
Not for PSEB/CBSE in Term-1

## M.C.Q – I (Detail explanation)

1. ___ refers to money and credit employed in the business.
    e) Business profit
    f) Financial services
    g) Business finance
    h) All the above

> Business finance refers to the money and credit employed in business firms.
> Answer: (C)

2. Which refers to acquisition and utilization of capital funds in meeting overall objective of business?
    e) Business finance
    f) Business profit
    g) Financial services
    h) Both a and c

> Business finance
> Answer: (A)

3. No business can survive without

e) Profit
f) Innovation
g) Goal
h) Finance

> Finance is called a life blood of business. Without profit, business still survive but without finances not possible.
> Answer: - (D)

4. The management that helps the business in procuring funds, investment of funds in short term and long term and distribution of surplus is called

i) Business management
j) Financial management
k) Planning management
l) HRM management

> Financial management is the management helps in all these.
> Answer: - (B)

5. Financial planning involves

a) Short term planning only
b) Long term planning only
c) Both short- and long-term planning
d) None of above

> Financial planning includes both the long-term and short-term planning.
> Answer: - (C)

6. The main objective of financial planning is

e) To ensure timely availability of finance
f) To ensure proper balance of finance
g) Both a and b
h) To ensure financial control

> Financial planning ensures both timely availability of funds and proper balance of the finance.
> Answer: - (C)

7. The proportion of the different long-term sources of finance is called:

e) Capitalization
f) Capital structure
g) Financial planning
h) Working capital

> Capital structure is the proportion of the different long-term sources of finance.
> Answer: - (B)

8. Which is not a type of long-term source
    e) Equity share capital
    f) Debentures
    g) Retained profits
    h) Public deposits

> Public deposits are the short-term and medium-term source of finance.
> Answer: - (D) Public deposits

9. The inclusion of the fixed cost capital along with equity share capital is called?
    e) Trading on equity
    f) Financial risk
    g) Debt structure
    h) Equity structure

> Trading on equity is the inclusion of fixed cost capital like debt and preference share along with equity share capital.
> Answer: - (A) Trading on equity.

10. What is the formula to calculate ROI?
    e) EAIT/Total investment
    f) EAIT/Gross investment
    g) EBIT/Total investment
    h) EBIT/Gross investment

> ROI = EBIT/Total investment
> Answer: - (C)

11. The capital which is used to purchase of fixed assets is called?
    e) Fixed capital
    f) Working capital
    g) Gross Capital.
    h) Net capital

> Fixed assets are for the long-term periods and fixed capital means the investment in purchase of fixed assets like land, furniture, machinery etc.
> Answer: (A)

12. Difference between current assets and current liabilities is called?

e) Fixed capital
f) Working capital
g) Gross capital
h) Net capital

> The working capital is the investment in current assets like cash, stock, debtors etc. The difference between current assets and current liabilities called as working capital
> Answer: - (B) working capital

13. Aggregate of current assets is
    e) Working capital
    f) Gross working capital
    g) Net working capital
    h) Net capital

> Aggregates of all the current assets of the firm is called as gross working capital.
> Answer: - (B)

14. Which is not a current asset?
    e) Marketable securities
    f) Prepaid expenses
    g) Provision for the bad debts
    h) Work in progress

> Every type of provision is the part of liabilities.
> Answer: - (c)

15. In which of following business working capital is more required?
    e) Manufacturing company
    f) Trading company
    g) Both a and b
    h) None of above

> Trading business means purchase and sale of goods but manufacturing means that make the quality product and hence need more working capital.
> Answer: - (A)

16. If textile company wants to do business of paper manufacturing the how much capital does company required as fixed?
    e) More
    f) Less
    g) Depend on area

h) Depend on layout

More because start of every business need purchase of land, machinery, furniture etc.
Answer: - (A)

17. Which is the costliest?
    e) Debentures
    f) Equity share capital
    g) Preference share capital
    h) All the above

Costliest is the Equity share capital of the company.
Answer: - (b)

18. Which is not a type of financial function?
    e) Investment decisions
    f) Finance decisions
    g) Asset decisions
    h) Dividend decisions

Finance function includes three decisions such as investment, finance and dividend. In short asset function is not the type of financial decisions.
Answer: - (C)

19. Which of following decisions means how the total funds required by business be obtained from various long-term sources?
    e) Finance decisions
    f) Investment decisions
    g) Dividend decisions
    h) Both a and b

Finance decisions means the decisions about how to arrange the funds for the business from long-term sources.
Answer: - (A)

20. The very important objective of the financial management is
    e) Profit maximization
    f) Wealth maximization
    g) Optimum utilization of funds
    h) Availability of funds at every time.

Financial management is more concerned about the one main objective is wealth maximization.

Answer: - (b)

21. To determine what is to be done in future is called
    e) Planning
    f) Financial planning
    g) Goals
    h) Forecasting

To determine about how the fund, arrange for future is called financial planning but its simple question what is to be done? So,
Answer: - (a)

22. Composition of liability side of balance sheet is called?
    a) Capital structure
    b) Financial structure
    c) Debt capital
    d) Capitalization

Answer: - (B)

23. How to calculate EPS?
    e) EAS/EBIT
    f) EBIT/EAS
    g) EAS/No. of equity shares
    h) EBIT* No. of equity shares

Answer: - (C)

24. To meet day-to-day expenses which capital is important?
    e) Fixed capital
    f) Gross working capital
    g) Net capital
    h) Working capital

Working capital means the capital for the short period of time and hence helps in meeting day-to-day expenses.
Answer: - (D)

25. If business have stable earnings then, what impact shows on dividend decisions?
    e) Positive impact

f) Negative impact
g) No impact
h) None of above

> If business have stable earnings, it means business has no problem to distribute the dividend.
> Answer: - (A)

# M.C.Q – II (Case Study Based)

1. Tanvi want to start their own business by investing the money in purchase of land, machinery, furniture etc. She wants to start their own trading business hence, required less amount of capital instead of manufacturing business. Identify the type of capital that highlighted above?

   a) Fixed capital
   b) Working capital
   c) Net capital
   d) Gross capital

> Answer: - (A)
> Hint: - start their own business by investing the money in purchase of land, machinery, furniture etc.

2. Suppose a company need Rs.10 Lakh. Company decided various sources of finance and then raise funds from it. Company decided to earn 45% of equity share capital, 22.50% from preference share capital, 11.25% from the borrowed capital, 11.25% from retained earnings and 10% of current liabilities. After that company completed their need.

Identify the concept discuss above.

   a) Capitalization

b) Capital structure
c) Financial structure
d) All the above

> Answer: - (B) Capital structure
>
> Hint to find Answer: - Capital structure is the composition of the different long-term sources of the capital.
>
> Note: - Students must remember the meaning of every concept during case studies.

3. A company takes debt of Rs100 and rate of interest on this debt is 10% and rate of tax is 30%. By deducting Rs10/- from the EBIT a saving of Rs.3/- in tax will take place. On the other hand, an interest of Rs10/- has been paid and Rs 3/- have been saved. Thus, real cost of debt is not 10% has been paid but only 7%. Similarly, if the rate of tax is 40%, the real cost of debt would be 6%.

Identify the factor that affect above (100% accurate)

a) Return on investment.
b) Cost of equity capital.
c) Debt service coverage ratio
d) Tax rate

> Answer: - (D) Tax rate
>
> Hint to get answer: - How debt helps in save tax or rate of tax affect.

4. A business that doesn't grow dies", says Mr. Shah, the owner of Shah Marble Ltd. with glorious 36 months of its grand success having a capital base of RS.80 crores. Within a short span of time, the company could generate cash flow which not only covered fixed cash payment obligations but also create sufficient buffer. The company is on the growth path and a new breed of consumers is eager to buy the Italian marble sold by Shah Marble Ltd. To meet the increasing demand, Mr. Shah decided to expand his business by acquiring a mine. This required an investment of RS.120 crores. To seek advice in this matter, he called his financial advisor Mr. Seth who advised him about the judicious mix of equity (40%) and Debt (60%). Mr. Seth also suggested him to take loan from a financial institution as the cost of raising funds from financial institutions is low. Though this will increase the financial risk but will also raise the return to equity shareholders. He also apprised him that issue of debt will not dilute the control of equity shareholders. At the same time, the interest on loan is a tax-deductible expense for computation of tax liability. After due deliberations with Mr. Seth, Mr. Shah decided to raise funds from a financial institution. Identify the concept of Financial Management as advised by Mr. Seth in the above situation.

a) Capitalization
b) Capital structure
c) Working capital
d) Fixed capital

Answer: - (B)

Hint to find answer: - the judicious mix of equity (40%) and Debt (60%).

5. Amit is running an 'advertising agency' and earning a lot by providing this service to big industries State whether the working capital requirement of the firm will be 'less' or 'more'.

Answer: - Less because he is running advertising agency which not need more inventory..

6. Apparels' is India's second largest manufacturer of branded Lifestyle apparel. The company now plans to diversify into personal care segment by launching perfumes, hair care and skin are products. Moreover, it is planning to open ten exclusive retail outlets in various cities across the country in next two years.
Identify the two factors affecting the fixed capital needs of the company.

- a) Growth prospects only
- b) Diversification only
- c) Both diversification and growth
- d) None of above

Answer: - (C)

- Hint: - Diversification: If a business enterprise plans to diversify into new product lines, its requirement of fixed capital will increase.
- Growth prospects: If a business enterprise plans to expand its current business operations in the anticipation of higher demand, consequently, more fixed capital will be needed by it

7. Khoo Surat Pvt. Ltd. is the largest hair salon chain in the Delhi, with over a franchise of 200 salons. The company is now planning to set up a manufacturing unit in Faridabad for production of various kinds of beauty products under its own brand name.
In context of the above case: Identify upon the fixed capital needs of the company.

- a) Low fixed capital
- b) High fixed capital
- c) Depend on business category
- d) None of above

Answer: - (a) Low fixed capital

Hint: - The fixed capital needs of the company are low as its salons have been promoted in the form of franchises.

8. Tata consultancy services is the largest trading company in the India. It is the biggest IT company in India and the second largest Indian company by Market capitalization. But from last few days they mostly concerned about their working capital earnings because boom period requires more working capital but on the other side competition level and raw material availability become the major issue in these days. But company as the largest in INDIA lead to overcome these very easily. Now tell, what main factors highlighted above

   a) Availability of raw material and competition.
   b) Competition, business cycle and growth prospectus
   c) Availability of raw material, business cycle and growth prospectus.
   d) Availability of raw material, kevel of competition and business cycle.

   Answer: - (D)

   Hint: - boom period requires more working capital but on the other side competition level and raw material availability become the major issue in these days.

9. A company wants to start a new unit in which machinery of worth Rs.10 lakh is involved. Identify the type of decision involved in financial requirements?

   a) Capital budgeting decisions.
   b) Short term investment decisions
   c) Financing decisions
   d) None of above.

   Answer: - (A) Capital budgeting decisions.

   Hint: -Capital budgeting decisions are also called long term investment decisions and invest in the fixed asset of firm.

10. Amisha is concerned about the funds raising from different sources. She plans to start and then firstly determine financial objective, then its policies, after that she decide to determine the procedures regarding the funds. As a result, she easily plans to raise the funds and then goals to be achieved. At last, she earns very good earnings after that. Tell, which process is highlighted above?

    a) Functional management
    b) Financial management
    c) Financial planning
    d) Capital structure.

    Answer: - (C)

    Hint: - Financial planning process involves: -

    - Determination of financial objective

- Determination of the financial policies
- Determination of financial procedures.

11. Reliance Co. is more actively want to increase the per share value of company. Choose from below, what point is highlighted above line.
    a) Profit maximization
    b) Wealth maximization
    c) Finance maximization
    d) Increase the availability of funds in the company.

Answer: - (B)

12. A company have two type of assets one is long-term and other is short-term. Now company in concerned about the selection of the asset suitable for them to invest because lot of factors that affecting them like cash flow position, rate of return, investment criteria etc.

Now tell, about which of following decisions management is concerned about?
    a) Financing decisions
    b) Dividend decisions
    c) Investment decisions
    d) None of above

Answer: - (C)
Investment decisions are the decisions that are relate to the selection of asset and then investment in it.

13. ABC Co. is the cloth trading company. Every year company earns very good earnings from sale of clothes but this year summers goes down and business have no sufficient earnings. Now winters comes and woolen clothes more needed. Company need best woolen clothes or the winter clothes to earn same return in this year as usual with last year. As for the same company have sufficient working capital but needs more. Now tell, what type of working capital company needs here or highlighted in above para.
    a) Initial working capital
    b) Regular working capital
    c) Seasonal working capital
    d) Special working capital

Answer: - (C) Seasonal working capital
Company needs working capital for winter season or particular season to earn best.

14. There are two companies which have their own different needs - Company A and B. Company A wants to invest in fixed assets of the firm to start their company with best earnings. While company B is running company and wants to meet their day to day expenses.

Now tell, which capital from following is used by company to satisfy their needs?

a) A and B both – Working capital
b) A – FIXED AND B – WORKING
c) A – WORKING AND B – FIXED
d) BOTH – FIXED

Answer: - (B) because fixed helps in purchasing fixed assets while working helps in meeting day to day expenses.

# M.C.Q – III (ASSERTION AND REASON)

ASSERTION(A): - Working capital is very important in every business.

REASON(R): - It helps in meeting the day to day expenses of the business.

Find the correct option: -

e) Both A and R are true and Reason is the correct explanation of Assertion.
f) Both A and R are true and R is not the correct explanation of A.
g) A is true and R is false.
h) A is false and R is true.

Working capital helps in meeting day to day expenses of the business. Hence, a very important in every business.
Answer: - (a) Both A and R are true and R is the correct explanation of A.

ASSERTION(A): - Fixed capital is the important capital need for every business.

REASON(R): - It helps in investing the money into fixed assets like machinery, furniture etc.

Find the correct option: -

e) Both A and R are true and Reason is the correct explanation of Assertion.
f) Both A and R are true and R is not the correct explanation of A.
g) A is true and R is false.
h) A is false and R is true.

> Fixed capital is that capital which is used to purchase fixed assets like machinery, furniture, building etc.
> Answer: - (A)

ASSERTION(A): - Working capital helps in addition in the value of business.

REASON(R): - It helps in timely payment of the all expenses and outstanding.

Find the correct option: -

   e) Both A and R are true and Reason is the correct explanation of Assertion.
   f) Both A and R are true and R is not the correct explanation of A.
   g) A is true and R is false.
   h) A is false and R is true.

> Working capital helps in timely payment of the dues or expenses. Hence also result in addition in the value of the business.
> Answer: - (A) Both A and R are true and R is correct explanation of A.

ASSERTION(A): - Every business not required funds to run their activities.

REASON(R): - Without profit, business will survive but without finance it is not possible.

Find the correct option: -

   e) Both A and R are true and Reason is the correct explanation of Assertion.
   f) Both A and R are true and R is not the correct explanation of A.
   g) A is true and R is false.
   h) A is false and R is true.

> Every business needs finance to run or survive. Business will run without profit for short period but without finance is not possible.
> Answer: - (D) A is false and R is true.

ASSERTION(A): - Most of the companies use debt capital more than equity because of less cost.

REASON(R): - Debt capital also have less risk more than equity.

Find the correct option: -

   e) Both A and R are true and Reason is the correct explanation of Assertion.
   f) Both A and R are true and R is not the correct explanation of A.
   g) A is true and R is false.
   h) A is false and R is true.

> Here A is true because Debt capital is used by lot of companies just because of its less raising cost. But it is riskier in nature than equity.

Answer: - (C) A is true but R is false.

ASSERTION(A): - Financial planning helps in facing eventualities.

REASON(R): -Financial planning refers to estimation of funds required in business to run the business smoothly.

Find the correct option: -

- e) Both A and R are true and Reason is the correct explanation of Assertion.
- f) Both A and R are true and R is not the correct explanation of A.
- g) A is true and R is false.
- h) A is false and R is true.

Here Both are true but R is not correct explanation of A. because R shows not the why but just the meaning of financial planning. So,
Answer: - (B) Both A and R are true and R is not the correct explanation of A.

ASSERTION(A): - Every business wants optimum financing decisions in their business.

REASON(R): - It results in minimum cost of capital.

Find the correct option: -

- e) Both A and R are true and Reason is the correct explanation of Assertion.
- f) Both A and R are true and R is not the correct explanation of A.
- g) A is true and R is false.
- h) A is false and R is true.

Answer: - (a) Both A and R are true and R is the correct explanation of A.

ASSERTION(A): - Every business requires finance.

REASON(R): - Profit is the life blood of every business.

Find the correct option: -

- e) Both A and R are true and Reason is the correct explanation of Assertion.
- f) Both A and R are true and R is not the correct explanation of A.
- g) A is true and R is false.
- h) A is false and R is true.

Yes, every business needs finance but profit is not life blood of business.

It's finance.
Answer: - (c) A is true and R is False.

ASSERTION(A): - Company dividend doesn't depend on the company earnings.

REASON(R): - The dividend is paid out of the present and reserve profits.

Find the correct option: -

a) Both A and R are true and Reason is the correct explanation of Assertion.
b) Both A and R are true and R is not the correct explanation of A.
c) A is true and R is false.
d) A is false and R is true.

> Earning is the main factor affecting the dividend decisions of the company and the dividend is paid out of the present and reserved profits.
>
> Answer: - (D) A is false and R is true.

# SOURCES OF FINANCE

(Special for ISC AND ICSE in Commerce)

Not for PSEB/CBSE in Term -1

## M.C.Q – I (Detail explanation)

1. The funds which are raised for the period of less then one year are called?
    a) Short tern funds
    b) Middle tern funds
    c) Long term funds
    d) None of above

> Short term funds – less than 1 year.
> Middle term funds – More than 1year or less than 5 year.
> Long term funds – More than 5 years.
> Answer: (A)

2. The funds raised through loans are called?

    a) Owner funds
    b) Borrowed funds
    c) Debt funds
    d) Long term funds

> Borrowed funds are the funds raised through loans.
> Answer: (B)

3. Which is the main source of owned funds?

    a) Retained earnings
    b) Equity shares
    c) Issue of debentures
    d) Both a and b

> Owned funds mean the funds invested by the owners of an enterprise.
> Answer: - (D)

4. Retained earnings are also called?

    a) Self-financing
    b) Ploughing back of profits
    c) Both a and b
    d) External financing

> Retained earnings are the internal source of business.
> It is called both the self-financing and ploughing back of profits.
> Answer: - (C)

5. Which of following is not the External source of funds?

    a) Preference shares
    b) Loan from bank
    c) Debentures
    d) Trade credit.

> Preference share is the internal source of funds that is raised within the organization.
> Answer: - (A)

6. The public deposits are regulated by
   a) Ministry of finance
   b) Commercial banks
   c) RBI
   d) All the above

Answer: - (C)

7. Equity shareholders are also called
   a) Owners of the company
   b) Partners of the company
   c) Executives of the company
   d) Guardian of the company

Equity shareholders are the owners of the company.
Answer: - (A)

8. Which is not a type of long-term source
   i) Equity share capital
   j) Debentures
   k) Retained profits
   l) Public deposits

Public deposits are the short-term and medium-term source of finance.
Answer: - (D) Public deposits

9. The term redeemable is used for
   a) Equity shares
   b) Preference shares
   c) Public deposits
   d) Commercial papers.

Redeemable preference shares are the shares that can be bought back by issuing company within pre-determined period.
Answer: - (B)

10. ADRs are issued by
    a) Canada
    b) China
    c) India
    d) USA

America issued ADRs i.e. American depository receipts.

Answer: - (D)

11. Debentures represents
    a) Fixed capital of the company
    b) Fluctuating capital of the company
    c) Permanent capital of the company
    d) Loan capital of the company

Debentures represents the loan capital of the company.
Answer: (D)

12. The maturity period of the commercial paper usually ranges from
    a) 20 to 40 days
    b) 120 days to 365 days
    c) 15days to 365 days
    d) 90 to 364 days

Answer: - (C)

13. An unsecured loan extended by one corporate to another.
    a) GDR
    b) ADR
    c) IDR
    d) ICD

Inter-corporate deposits are the deposits that are extended by one corporate to another.
Answer: - (D)

14. Which is the medium-term source of funds?
    a) Public deposits
    b) Equity shares
    c) Trade credits
    d) Preference shares

Answer: - (A)

15. The debentures which do not carry any charge on the assets of the company.
    a) Bearer debentures
    b) Secured debentures
    c) Unsecured debentures

d) Second debentures

Answer: - (C)

16. Dividend is paid only on
   a) Loan
   b) Bonds
   c) Shares
   d) Debentures

The return on shares is called dividend.
Answer: - (C)

17. Interest is paid only on
   a) Shares
   b) Loan
   c) Debentures
   d) ICD

Issue of debentures give a return of interest.
Answer: - (C)

18. The company divided the share capital into small parts called?
   a) Capital
   b) Authorized capital
   c) Shares
   d) Equity shares

The capital of the company is divided into small parts called shares.
Answer: - (C)

19. The nominal value of preference shares are generally
   a) High
   b) Low
   c) Depend on type of company

The nominal value of preference shares are generally higher than equity shares.
Answer: - (A)

20. The company issue rights shares generally to?
   a) All shareholders
   b) New shareholders
   c) Existing shareholder

d) None of above

> The Right Shares refers to the shares that are issued offered to existing shareholders of the company.
> Answer: - (C)

21. In which of following scheme, shareholders buy the specified number of shares at low less than market price.

   a) Employee buying shares options
   b) Employee shares options
   c) Employee low price shares
   d) Employee stock option plan

> ESOP – Employee Stock Option Plans.
> Answer: - (D)

22. Which of following shares are issued by the company under section 79A?

   a) Right shares
   b) Bonus shares
   c) Sweat equity shares
   d) Equity shares

Answer: - (C)

23. Which source of fund also called account receivable financing?

   a) Installment credit
   b) Factoring
   c) Customer advances
   d) Inter corporate deposits.

Answer: - (B)

# M.C.Q – II (Case Study Based)

1. Amisha Panwar is a Chartered Accountant. After completing her CA with top rank, she become the FRM- Financial Risk Manager designed by Global Associations of Risk Management. She firstly uses their own money but recently she needed loan from bank to use it as in most professional way. She did all things in very nice way.

Choose from the selection below – the external finance she used is which type of finance?

   a) Short-term source of finance
   b) Medium-term source of finance
   c) Long-term source of finance
   d) All the above

Answer: - (D)

Hint: - She uses loan from commercial bank and it is short-term, middle-term and as well as long-term source of finance.

2. Qureshi has aspired to start a Thai food restaurant from his childhood. On completing his education, he shared his childhood dream with his father. Therefore, the father-son duo decided to approach a nearby bank to obtaining a loan. His father's foremost concern was to raise the funds for the business as his savings would be insufficient for starting a business.

Which of following concept is discussed in above para?

   a) Financial planning
   b) Trade credit
   c) Business finance
   d) Industrial finance.

Answer: - (B) Capital structure

Hint to find Answer: - Business finance means the finance required by business to run their activities is called business finance.

3. Gracious Ltd. I a US based company. The company plans to tap the Indian Capital Market through its forthcoming issue of equity shares.

Choose from below, which instrument is used by company to raise funds from Indian capital market?

   a) ADRs
   b) GDRs
   c) IDRs
   d) ICDs

Answer: - (C)

Hint to get answer: - IDRs- Indian depository receipt is issued to raise money from Indian capital market.
ADRs – American depository receipts – only issue to raise money from American capital market.
GDRs stands for global depository receipts – issue to every country except America.

4. Gunjan Cinemas is a popular film entertainment company in Delhi. Keeping in view the growing culture of multiplex its owners have decided to make some changes in the interiors. The company wants to raise funds for the period of more than one year but less than 5 years.

Identify the funds type- that Gunjan seeks to raise on basis of time period.
- a) Short-term finance
- b) Medium-term finance
- c) Long-term finance
- d) None of above.

Answer: - (B)

Hint to find answer: - The company wants to raise funds for the period of more than one year but less than 5 years.

5. Rakesh plans to set up an environment friendly textile factory. He plans to use fossil fuels to make paint, plastics and polymers. Since the waste water from textile processing and dyeing contain residues, he has also decided to ensure its appropriate treatment before it is released into environment. He is planning to approach a Special Financial Institutions to raise loans.

Which of the following will he choose?
- a) ICICI
- b) IFCI
- c) UTI
- d) All the above

Answer: - (d) because all are the special financial institutions.

6. Ding Dong Ltd. is planning to float an issue of equity shares in the market in next four months. The directors of the company are also of the opinions that the company should raise some portion of funds from international capital market through equity.

Tell, which of following company will use to raise the funds from international capital market?
- a) ADRs

b) GDRs
c) IDRs
d) ICDs

Answer: - (B)

International capital market does not mention America, so its just GDRS because USA has its own raising sources.

7. Recently when Mosaic Ltd. was failing short of funds to meet the floatation cost of its upcoming issue of preference shares, the company raised deposits from Rosaic Ltd. which has surplus funds. Which source of fund highlighted above?

   a) ICDs
   b) ADRs
   c) Trade Credit
   d) Public deposits

Answer: - (a)ICDs – Inter Corporate deposits

Hint: - the company raised deposits from Rosaic Ltd. which has surplus funds.

8. Ayasha is successfully running a bakery shop in her residential colony for past many years. She had wisely invested funds in different areas in order to ensure smooth functioning of her business. She owns manufacturing unit, whereas the shop through which she operates is on rent. Recently she took a loan from the bank to install air conditioners. Although she buys majority of the ingredients like flour, sugar, oil on 15 days credit from local supplier but sales are only made in cash.

Which two external sources of funds highlighted above

   a) Loan from bank and loan from financial institution.
   b) Loan from bank and trade credit
   c) Loan from bank and ICDs
   d) ICDs and trade credit.

Answer: - (b)
Hint: - she took a loan from the bank to install air conditioners. – loan from bank
Although she buys majority of the ingredients like flour, sugar, oil on 15 days credit from local supplier but sales are only made in cash. – Trade credit

9. A new setup company needs finance to purchase fixed capital and for the period of maximum 10 years.

Tell which source of finance discuss above?

   a) Long-term source of finance
   b) Short-term source of finance

c) Medium-term source of finance.
d) All the above

Answer: - (A) Long-term source of finance.

Hint: - Long-term funds have period of more than 5 years.

10. Sachin Arora is the businessman that runs a business of jewelry. He noticed that demand for jewelry increases day by day. He decided to increases his jewelry stock also. He takes a loan from the IFCI institution so that he will earn maximum profits.

a) Loan from bank
b) Loan from financial institution
c) Trade Credit
d) Issue Preference shares

Answer: - (B)

- Hint: - a loan from the IFCI. IFCI is a financial institution.

11. Taste Buds is the well reputed company in India. Company just analyze the books and found out that they have very much undistributed profits. Company decided that it must be distributed to all shareholders as dividend but Amisha, one of the female BOD and Sachin one of the male BOD of company, suggested them to issue fully paid shares to them free of charge in proportion of existing shareholders instead of dividend. Now tell,

About which of following shares, Amisha and Sachin suggested to company?

a) Bonus shares
b) Rights shares
c) Equity shares
d) Sweat equity shares.

Answer: - (A)
Bonus shares means the fully paid shares issued to shareholders free of charge.

12. Star Ltd issued already many equity and preference shares to subscribe for public and earns lot of profits and earnings. But company thinks not fit with that earnings and want to further issue the shares, but now first to their existing shareholders and then further think.

No tell, which of following type of share highlighted above?

a) Bonus shares
b) Sweat equity shares
c) Equity shares

d) Right issue/ shares

> Answer: - (D)
> Whenever company comes out with further issue of shares and they must first offer to their existing shareholders are called Right issue/ shares.

# M.C.Q – III (ASSERTION AND REASON)

ASSERTION(A): - ICDs are not convenient and popular now a days.

REASON(R): - It is because of no legal formalities are involved.

Find the correct option: -

a) Both A and R are true and Reason is the correct explanation of Assertion.
b) Both A and R are true and R is not the correct explanation of A.
c) A is true and R is false.
d) A is false and R is true.

> ICDs are popular and convenient only because of the no legal formalities.
> Answer: - (D) A is false and R is True.

ASSERTION(A): - Factoring is the expensive method to raise funds.

REASON(R): - It is because it is sold at very high discounts.

Find the correct option: -

a) Both A and R are true and Reason is the correct explanation of Assertion.
b) Both A and R are true and R is not the correct explanation of A.
c) A is true and R is false.
d) A is false and R is true.

> Factoring is the best method to raise funds in company. But is too expensive because of sold at heavy discounts.
> Answer: - (A) Both A and R are true and R is the correct explanation of A.

ASSERTION(A): - Trade credit is more economical than banks.

REASON(R): - It is because interest charge at low rate.

Find the correct option: -

a) Both A and R are true and Reason is the correct explanation of Assertion.
b) Both A and R are true and R is not the correct explanation of A.
c) A is true and R is false.
d) A is false and R is true.

> Trade credit is economical than bank loans because no interest charge.
> Answer: - (C) A is True and R is False.

ASSERTION(A): - Interest paid on debentures allowed at deduction in Income tax.

REASON(R): - It results in tax relief.

Find the correct option: -

a) Both A and R are true and Reason is the correct explanation of Assertion.
b) Both A and R are true and R is not the correct explanation of A.
c) A is true and R is false.
d) A is false and R is true.

> Answer: - (A) Both A and R are true and R is the correct explanation of A.

ASSERTION(A): - More retained earnings results in more investment by shareholders.

REASON(R): - More ploughing back of profits gives dissatisfaction to the shareholders.

Find the correct option: -

a) Both A and R are true and Reason is the correct explanation of Assertion.
b) Both A and R are true and R is not the correct explanation of A.
c) A is true and R is false.
d) A is false and R is true.

> More retained earnings result in dissatisfaction among shareholders. Hence, they don't make to like invest more and more in the company.
> Answer: - (D) A is true and R is false.

ASSERTION(A): - Sweat Equity Shares are not issued under a formal scheme.

REASON(R): -These shares are issued under section 79A of Companies Act, 1956.

Find the correct option: -
a) Both A and R are true and Reason is the correct explanation of Assertion.
b) Both A and R are true and R is not the correct explanation of A.
c) A is true and R is false.
d) A is false and R is true.

Sweat equity shares are issued under section 79A and also not issued under formal scheme but here the reason is not perfect explanation because its perfect explanation is that it not issue at any time just for formal scheme.
Answer: - (B) Both A and R are true and R is not the correct explanation of A.

ASSERTION(A): - Right shares brings cash to the company's coffers.

REASON(R): - The shares of right issue are fully paid-up.

Find the correct option: -
a) Both A and R are true and Reason is the correct explanation of Assertion.
b) Both A and R are true and R is not the correct explanation of A.
c) A is true and R is false.
d) A is false and R is true.

Right shares are not fully paid-up shares and hence brings cash to company's coffers. It shows that
Answer: - (C) A is true and R is false.

ASSERTION(A): - Bonus shares are partial paid-up shares.

REASON(R): - Bonus shares are also called capitalization of undistributed profits of a company.

Find the correct option: -
a) Both A and R are true and Reason is the correct explanation of Assertion.
b) Both A and R are true and R is not the correct explanation of A.
c) A is true and R is false.
d) A is false and R is true.

Bonus shares are called capitalization of undistributed profits but it is fully-paid up shares not partial
Answer: - (D) A is false and R is true.

ASSERTION(A): - There is no trading on equity in case of equity shares.

REASON(R): - Because the entire amount of the share capital is raised through equity shares.

Find the correct option: -

a) Both A and R are true and Reason is the correct explanation of Assertion.
b) Both A and R are true and R is not the correct explanation of A.
c) A is true and R is false.
d) A is false and R is true.

Answer: - (A) Both A and R true and R is the correct explanation of A.

# BANKING – LATEST TRENDS

(Special for ISC AND ICSE in Commerce)

Not for CBSE AND PSEB in Term -1

# M.C.Q – I (Detail explanation)

1. The specialist funds transfer system where transfer of funds take place from one bank to another on gross basis.
    a) RTGS
    b) NEFT
    c) Both a and b
    d) IMPS

Answer: (A)

2. What is the minimum amount of RTGS?
    a) 1 LAKH
    b) 2 LAKHS
    c) 3 LAKHS
    d) 50 THOUSAND

Answer: (B)

3. In RTGS, Real Time means
    a) Waiting period
    b) No waiting periods
    c) Payment period
    d) None of above

Real time means there is no waiting period.
Answer: - (B)

4. RTGS services available to customer on week days in between
    a) 9am to 12pm
    b) 9am to 3pm
    c) 9am to 2pm
    d) 9am to 2.30pm

Time period RTGS in week: -
9am to 3pm

ON SATURDAY
9am to 12pm.
Answer: - (B)

5. RTGS is only enabled by which bank branches?
    a) CBR enabled banks

b) CBS enabled banks
c) SBS enabled banks
d) CB enabled banks

CBS – Core banking enabled banks use RTGS.
Answer: - (B)

6. What is the fees to be charged on RTGS by banks?

   a) Rs. 50
   b) RS. 100
   c) Rs. 200
   d) Vary from bank to bank

Answer: - (D)

7. During week days, NEFT take place

   a) 2 times a day
   b) 3 times a day
   c) 4 times a day
   d) 6 times a day

6 times a day: - 9am, 10.30am, 12noon, 1pm, 3pm and 4pm
Answer: - (D)

8. If someone not have bank account then the maximum amount transferred from NEFT is

   a) 29999
   b) 39999
   c) 49999
   d) 59999

Answer: - (C)49999

9. What is normally minimum value to transfer through NEFT?

   a) 2lakhs
   b) 3lakhs
   c) 5lakhs
   d) No minimum value

There is no minimum value in case of NEFT.
Answer: - (D)

10. Which card is used to make payment from ATM also?

a) Debit card
b) Credit card
c) Both a and b
d) Only ATM card – No other card

> You can use debit card to withdrew money from ATM machine.
> Answer: - (A)

11. Which of following the type of cheques drawn by bank either on its branch or on another bank in favor of third party?

a) Cash Credit documents
b) Bank draft
c) Promissory note
d) Bill of exchange

Answer: (B)

12. which of the following is the banking latest- trend?

a) SMS alert
b) Tele-banking
c) CBS
d) All the above.

Answer: - (D)

# MARKETING

(Special for PSEB AND CBSE in term -1 & several boards)
NOT for the ISC AND ICSE in term -1 in Commerce subject

## M.C.Q – I (DETAIL EXPLANATION)

1. The process under which valuable goods/services are created, offered and by doing transaction independently, the needs are satisfied.
   a) Marketing
   b) Marketing planning
   c) Marketing Mix
   d) All the above.

   Answer: - (A)

2. Scope of _____ is limited but scope of _____ is wider.
   a) Marketing, Selling
   b) Selling, Marketing
   c) Marketing, Publicity
   d) Selling, Manufacturing

   Selling is the part of marketing. Hence, narrow in scope.
   Answer: - (b)

3. Which philosophies of marketing related to the cheap goods available all time and cannot create problem in sale?
   a) Product concept\
   b) Production concept
   c) Marketing concept
   d) Societal Marketing concept

   Answer: - (b)

4. Which of following need to pay attention to promotion?
   a) Marketing mix
   b) Marketing
   c) Selling
   d) Product concept

   Marketing focuses on the product, promotion, pricing and physical distribution. So,

Answer: - (C)

5. What is the main aim of the Selling concept of marketing philosophies?
   a) Quality of product
   b) Availability of product
   c) Attracting customers
   d) Consumer satisfaction

> Production concept: - Quantity of product
> Product concept: - Quality of product
> Selling concept: - Attracting consumers
> Marketing concept: - Consumer satisfaction
> Societal concept: - Consumer welfare.
>
> Answer: - (C)

6. Which of following not starts from factory?
   a) Product concept
   b) Production concept
   c) Marketing concept
   d) Selling Concept

> Marketing concept starts from the market.
> Answer: - (C)

7. Who is not a part of one level channel?
   a) Consumer
   b) Retailer
   c) Manufacturer
   d) Wholesaler

> One channel includes: -
> Manufacturer to Retailer and then to consumer. No wholesaler.
> Answer: - (D)

8. Which of following is part of marketing mix?
   a) Product
   b) Price
   c) Promotion and place
   d) All the above

Answer: - (D)

9. The combination of all decisions related to make the product available to consumers?
   a) Product mix
   b) Place mix
   c) Price mix
   d) Promotion mix

Answer: - (B)

10. Publicity is a part of which of following?
    a) Price mix
    b) Promotion mixes
    c) Product mix
    d) Place mix

Publicity is the promotion and hence come under the Promotion mixes.

Answer: - (B)

11. Packing is the part of which 4P?
    a) Product
    b) Price
    c) Place
    d) Promotion

We pack the products. Hence,
Answer: - (A)

12. Is labeling Compulsory?
    a) Depend on producer
    b) Yes
    c) No
    d) None of above.

Answer: - Compulsory by government. Yes (B)

13. What does Grade label shows?
    a) Brand of the product
    b) Description level
    c) Quality of product
    d) Batch No.

Answer: - (C)

14. LUX is a
   a) Label
   b) Packing
   c) Brand
   d) Trade mark

Answer: - (C)

15. Introducing a scheme of 50% + 40% less by the KOUTONS is the example of which sales promotion technique?
   a) Rebate
   b) Discount
   c) Refunds
   d) Full Finance

Under rebate, in order to clear the stock the excess stock products are offered at reduced price.

Under Discount, the customers are offered products on less than the listed prices.
Answer: - (B)

16. Which of following is full personal?
   a) Publicity
   b) Advertising
   c) Personal selling
   d) Sales promotion

Answer: - (C) Personal selling

17. What is "Watch repair?"
   a) Product
   b) Perishable product
   c) Durable product
   d) Services

Answer: - (D) Services

18. How many levels of packaging have?
   a) 1
   b) 2
   c) 3
   d) 4

3 levels: - Primary, Secondary, and Transportation
Answer: - (c) 3

19. Which of following is not concerned with price?
   a) Advertising
   b) List price
   c) Margins
   d) Discounts

   Answer: - (A)

20. SWOT analysis is the main part of the
   a) Selling
   b) Production
   c) Marketing
   d) Publicity

   It is the main part of marketing concept where all factors are concerned.
   Answer: - (C)

21. Under marketing, which of following is not the product?
   a) Quality
   b) List price
   c) Design
   d) Label

   Quality, Design and label are the parts of the products and hence, list price not come under it.
   Answer: - (B)

22. Which of following is not the part of "Place and Promotion."
   a) Advertising
   b) Warranties
   c) Personal selling
   d) Sales Promotion

   Place and promotion mean goods to promote and reach to customers. Hence, advertising, personal selling, sales promotion is come under it.
   Answer: - (B)

23. Providing information to the customers about the product, its features and quality etc.

a) Production
b) Pricing
c) Promotion
d) None of above

Answer: - (C)

24. Discounts, rebate, free samples are come under: -

a) Publicity
b) Advertising
c) Personal selling
d) Sales promotion

All are the methods for sales promotion.

Answer: - (D)

25. _____ activities start after the product has been developed?

a) Selling
b) Publicity
c) Marketing

ANSWER: - (A) Selling

## M.C.Q – II (CASE STUDY BASED)

1. Yogesh buys a new laptop for his son Mukesh on his birthday from company retail outlet. After a few months, some parts of laptop get damaged in 3 road accidents. Yogesh approaches the deals to get damaged parts replaced with new ones. But, he told that the company does not provide any after sale services to customers. Yogesh feels dissatisfied as a consumer and think to not buy any product from this company again ever in life. In the context above, tell which function of marketing here ignored by company?

a) Labelling
b) Customer support services
c) Customer dealings.
d) Proper management of product.

Here the company not to provide after sale service to their customers. It shows that company properly deal with customers in selling product but their support services to customers lacking here.

Answer: - (B)

2. Suraj is a small entrepreneur involved in the manufacturing of hair wax. He finds that cost of production of 100gm of hair wax is Rs. 250. He has decided to keep a margin of 15% as profit. Moreover, he has assessed that there is a free competition in this product segment.

Identify the function of marketing being performed by Suraj.

   a) Decide cost of product
   b) Pricing of product
   c) Decision about product
   d) Margin requirements in product.

> Suraj finds COP of 100gm of hair wax Rs. 250 – shows that he is deciding about the price of product to be charged.
> Answer: - (B)

3. As a number of people making online purchases has increased manifold, there is a growing concern about the disposal and management of packaging waste. Every item bought is delivered with excess packaging and sometimes even non-biodegradable materials are used.

Choose the two other level that marketers may using besides immediate package.

   a) Primary and secondary packaging
   b) Secondary and transportation packaging
   c) Primary and transportation packaging
   d) None of above

> Packaging are of three types: - Primary, secondary and transportation.
> So, Immediate packaging means the primary packaging. After that two others are
> Answer: - (B)

4. As a global leader in consumer electronics and entertainment industries, Sony has set forth 'Road to Zero environmental plan' to achieve a zero-environment effect by year 2050 by producing world-class products in a manner that both products and promotes a healthy and sustainable planet.

Identify the market philosophy being implemented by company.

   a) Product
   b) Production
   c) Marketing
   d) Societal

> Societal philosophy means the philosophy which main focus is on both the need of potential buyers as well as concern for society at large.

Showing above --- Sony has set forth 'Road to Zero environmental plan' to achieve a zero-environment effect by year 2050 by producing world-class products in a manner that both products and promotes a healthy and sustainable planet.

Answer: - (D)

5. Ranger India Limited, is an automobile manufacturer in India. It makes 1.5 million family cars every year. That's one car every 12 seconds. It has a sales network of company approved retailers that spreads across 600 cities.

Now choose which channel of distribution adopted by the company?

   a) Direct channel
   b) Three level Channel
   c) Two level Channel
   d) One level Channel

Manufacturer – retailers --- consumers
Answer: - (D) One level Channel

6. Mansi, a shoe manufacturer for school students, decided to maximize profits by producing and distributing shoes on a large-scale and thus reducing the average cost of production. Identify market management philosophy adopted by Mansi.

   a) Product
   b) Marketing
   c) Production
   d) Selling

Production philosophy has main focus on quantity of product produced.

Hint: - decided to maximize profits by producing and distributing shoes on a large-scale and thus reducing the average cost of production.

Answer: - (C)

7. Amar is engaged in manufacturing of refrigerators. He surveyed the market and found that customers need a refrigerator with a separate provision of water cooler in it. He decided and launched the same refrigerator in the market.

Choose from below the market philosophy discuss in above para.

   a) Marketing
   b) Societal
   c) Product
   d) Selling

Surveyed the market --- shows that we touched and focus mainly on marketing.

Hence,
Answer: - (A)

8. Zoom Udyog, a car manufacturing company, has started its business with zoom-800 and slowly launched Zoom-800, Wagon-Z, Swy-fy etc. and offered various services like after sales services, availability of spare parts, etc.

Identify element of marketing mix referred here.

   a) Price
   b) Place
   c) Promotion
   d) Product

Above para not shows any price or advertising material or not discuss about place. So, in short simple to say by understanding the line that whole para discusses about product.
Answer: - (D)

9. Ankita took her niece Ritika for shopping to Mega Stores to buy her a bag for her birthday. She was delighted when on payment of bag she got a pencil box along with bag as free of cost.

Identify the technique of sales promotion used by company.

   a) Rebate
   b) Discount
   c) Free sample
   d) Product combination

Answer: - (D)

10. Amisha is the manager of the company. Her main area of focus is to generate revenue for the company through repeated sales. He decides to develop a product for the company which can generate revenue in long run. For this he meets a team a team of R&D of his company. After a long meeting they decide to do survey. Based on survey a product made to fulfil needs of customers. The product later produces a lot of revenue through repeated sales in long run.

Identify the market philosophy.

   a) Product
   b) Production
   c) Marketing
   d) Selling

Students not confuse here that whole para is about product. But here we do survey also and its come under the marketing philosophy and hence

Answer: - (C)

11. Krishna is the distributer to far off places. He has opened a company which deals in tea selling. He has categories his tea to be sold into three categories. Green, yellow and red. His brother Ramesh running a mobile manufacturing company. His company strictly produces mobile according to the pre-determined specifications. The mobiles of each variety are of same size, looks and performance.

Which function of marketing highlighted above

   a) Branding
   b) Grading and packaging
   c) Grading and labelling and market research
   d) Grading and standardization.

Answer: - (D)

12. Automobiles Ltd. offered to sell their new bike at about Rs. 4000 less than the usual price. It is an example of

   a) Rebate
   b) Discount
   c) Sale Sale
   d) None of these.

Rebate means sold goods at low price to clear excess stock.
Discount means offered the product at price less than listed price.
Answer: - (B)

13. A Consumer product manufacturing company is offering a number of consumer products like toiletries, detergent powder, food products etc. Identify 1 element of marketing mix.

   a) Price
   b) Promotion
   c) Place
   d) Product

Answer: - (D)

14. Shalu purchased a bottle of tomato-sauce from the local grocery shop. The information provided on the bottle was not clear. She fell sick by consuming it. She filed a case in the District forum under consumer protection act and got relief.

Identify the important aspect that neglected by marketer in above case?

   a) Branding
   b) Packaging

c) Labelling
d) None of above.

> Labelling refers to process of preparing a label.
> Above case shown that information on bottle was not clear---- it means label.
> Answer: - (C)

15. Amitabh Bachchan, the legendary Bollywood actor is often seen in a television advertisement of Gujrat tourism. In this particular advertisement he encourages people to visit Gujrat and spend more time there by quoting line "KUCHH DIN TOH GUZARO GUJRAT MEIN". Identify what being marketed by Mr. Amitabh Bachchan in above case.
    a) Price about product
    b) Place
    c) Product information
    d) Promotion of product

> Answer: - (B)- Not promotion because all para is about place totally not product promotion.

# SAMPLE PAPERS

## SAMPLE PAPER – I (CBSE)

Sample Question Paper 2021-22

Term 1
Subject: Business Studies
Time: 90 minutes
Max. Marks: 40

General instructions:
1. The Question Paper contains 3 sections.
2. Section A has 24 questions. Attempt any 20 questions.
3. Section B has 24 questions. Attempt any 20 questions.
4. Section C has 12 questions. Attempt any 10 questions.
5. All questions carry equal marks.
6. There is NO negative marking.

## Section – A

**1.** Which concept have main focus on cost?

   A. Effectiveness
   B. Efficiency
   C. Both a and b
   D. Management

**2.** Management is _____ directed process as it aims at achieving specified goals.

   A. Continuously
   B. Future
   C. Goal
   D. Deliberately.

**3.** Identify the feature of coordination being highlighted in given statement. Coordination is not a one-time function, it begins at the planning stage and continue till controlling.

   A. Coordination ensures unity of action.
   B. Coordination is an all-pervasive function
   C. Coordination is a continuous process
   D. Coordination is a deliberate function.

**4.** _____ involves harmony and team spirit among employees.

   A. Discipline
   B. Esprit de corps

|   |   |
|---|---|
|   | C. Order<br>D. Standardization |
| 5. | The health and fitness trend have become popular among large number of urban dwellers. This created a demand for products like organic food, this is an example of:<br><br>A. Customs and Traditions<br>B. Values<br>C. Social Trends<br>D. All of these |
| 6. | What resources are specially kept in view in planning?<br><br>A. Limited<br>B. Unlimited<br>C. Both a and b<br>D. None of these |
| 7. | "In case the debts are not paid within a month interest at a definite rate will be levied." To what element of planning does this saying point out?<br><br>A. Policy<br>B. Rule<br>C. Procedure<br>D. Budget. |
| 8. | Name the process which coordinated human efforts, assembles resources and integrated both into a unified whole to be utilized for achieving specified objectives.<br><br>A. Management<br>B. Organizing<br>C. Planning<br>D. Coordination |
| 9. | Identify the type of organizational structure which facilitates occupational specialization.<br><br>A. Functional |

|     |     |
| --- | --- |
|     | B. Horizontal<br>C. Network<br>D. Divisional |
| 10. | Which is not the element of delegation?<br><br>A. Responsibility<br>B. Authority<br>C. Decentralization<br>D. Accountability |
| 11. | When decision-making authority is retained organization is said to be by higher management levels, an<br><br>A. Decentralized<br>B. Centralized<br>C. Fragmented<br>D. None of above |
| 12. | Providing finance at 0%. Which of following adopts this method?<br><br>A. Advertisement<br>B. Personal selling<br>C. Sales promotion<br>D. Publicity |
| 13. | Customer satisfaction alone can ensure success. Which marketing hold this view?<br><br>A. Production concept.<br>B. Product concept<br>C. Marketing concept<br>D. Selling concept |
| 14. | Under which of following conditions does a business need not maintain high level of inventory?<br><br>A. When higher level of customer services needs to provided.<br>B. When high degree of accurate sales forecast can be made.<br>C. When the responsiveness of the distribution system is low. |

|   |   |
|---|---|
|   | D. All of above |
| 15. | Under the concept of "Marketing management" marketing is done keeping ___ as a focus: -<br><br>A. Consumer<br>B. Supplier<br>C. Investor<br>D. None of above. |
| 16. | Planning strangulates the initiative of the employees and compels them to work in the inflexible manner. **What does it mean?**<br><br>A. Planning is rigid in nature<br>B. Planning reduces creativity<br>C. Planning does not work in dynamic environment.<br>D. Both a and b |
| 17. | Just after Lok Sabha declaration elections 2009 results, the Bombay stock Exchange price index rose by 2100 points in a day. **Identify the environment factor which led to rise**<br><br>A. Environment of economics.<br>B. Environment of politics.<br>C. Environment of legal.<br>D. All of above. |
| 18. | For which type of organization is scientific management useful?<br><br>A. Small organizations<br>B. Large organizations<br>C. Both small and large organizations<br>D. None |
| 19. | Hina and Harish are typists in a company having the same educational qualification. Hina is getting Rs. 3000 per month and Harish Rs. 4000 per month for same working hours. **Which principle of management is violated here?**<br><br>A. Equity |

| | |
|---|---|
| | B. Initiative<br>C. Fair remuneration to workers.<br>D. Esprit de crops |
| 20. | "In order to be successful an organization must change its goals according to the needs of the environment." **Which characteristic of management is highlighted in the element?**<br><br>A. Management is pervasive.<br>B. Management is dynamic.<br>C. Management is goal-oriented.<br>D. Management is group efforts. |
| 21. | Anything minus management is nothing. What this shows:<br><br>A. Limitation of management<br>B. Nature of management<br>C. Importance of management<br>D. Scope of management. |
| 22. | At what level coordination required?<br><br>A. At top level.<br>B. At middle level.<br>C. At low level<br>D. At all levels of management. |
| 23. | Different techniques were developed by Taylor to facilitate principles of scientific management. One of them is fatigue study. **What is the objective of this study?**<br><br>A. Maintain the work time.<br>B. Maintain the rest-intervals<br>C. Maintain the efficiency levels of workers<br>D. Maintain the time intervals of employees during workers. |
| 24. | Does mere planning ensure success?<br><br>A. Yes<br>B. No |

| | | |
|---|---|---|
| | | C. Doesn't say |
| | | SECTION-B |
| 25. | | Jay is working as a marketing manager in a company. Has been given task of selling 100000 units of products at the cost of Rs. 100 per unit within 20 days. He is able to sell all the units within the stipulated time, but had to sell last 1000 units at 20% discount in order to complete the target. **In such a situation, he will be considered to be**<br><br>A. An efficient manager.<br>B. An effective manager<br>C. Both effective and efficient.<br>D. None of above. |
| 26. | | Mansi took her niece Ridhima for shopping to Mega stores to buy her a bag for her birthday. She was delighted when on payment of the bag she got a pencil box along with the bag free of cost. **Identify the techniques of sales promotion used by the company.**<br><br>A. Discount<br>B. Rebate<br>C. Free gifts<br>D. Product combination. |
| 27. | | Kiran industries is a company dealing in office furniture. The company chose to diversify its operations to improve its growth potential and increase market share, As a project was important, many alternatives were generated for the purpose. After evaluating the various alternatives, Sukhvinder, the Managing Director of the company, decided they should add "Home interiors and furnishings" as a new line of business activity. **Identify the name of framework, which the diversified organization should adopt, to enable it to cope with emerging complexity?**<br><br>A. Divisional organization<br>B. Functional organization<br>C. Rational organization<br>D. Informal organization. |
| 28. | | Amisha is a bright young management trainee. After sixth months of the testing |

by her organization she is given charge of her office as an assistant manager. She starts her job with a lot of enthusiasm but realizes that it won't be possible for her to continue without sharing her tasks. She keeps a secretary who takes order from her. This has reduced her burden of work and has helped her to focus on priority assignment.
**Which concept of management is discussed in above case?**

    A. Decentralization
    B. Delegation
    C. Centralization
    D. Organization.

29. Ramesh is a senior middle level manager. He is busy in allocating resources to his staff, he has also finalized the objectives and decided the course of action to be followed. He is expecting energy in his staff for the whole session but he will have to be caucious.
**Identify the type of plan.**

    A. Objective
    B. Strategy
    C. Policy
    D. Method

30. A specific statement was given by HR Head. This statement had no scope for any flexibility. It was the simplest type of plan. **Identify the type of plan.**

    A. Programme
    B. Rule
    C. Policy
    D. Procedure

31. ABC ltd. is engaged in producing electricity from domestic garbage. There is almost equal division of work and responsibilities between the workers and the management. The management even takes workers into confidence before taking important decisions. All the workers are satisfied as the behavior of the management is very good.
**Which of following principle of management highlighted above?**

    A. Harmony not discords
    B. Corporate not individualism

C. Division of work
D. Esprit de crops.

**32.** "Study Buddy Pvt. Ltd." is a company dealing in stationary items. In order to establish standards of excellence and quality in material and in performance of men and machines, the company adheres to benchmarks during production. Moreover, its products are available in limited varieties, sizes and dimensions thereby eliminating superfluous diversity of products.
**Identify the technique of scientific management which has been adopted by company?**

A. Method study
B. Fatigue study
C. Simplification and standardization
D. Functional foremanship

**33.** A scientist working in a factory for the betterment of operational aspect studied all the steps involved in the manufacturing of the product. He is very attentively noticed all sorts of movements to arrive at a simpler way of doing all the activities possible. With this hard work he was able to bring down the number of activities for the manufacturing of final product from 34 to 22. This work was decreasing the total time of production. Thus, he gave the organization an added advantage.
**Which type of scientific technique is discussed here.**

A. Method study
B. Motion study
C. Time study
D. Standardization

**34.** Pokka employment is a company which takes care the fact that the confidence of the employees should always be at its peak. For this reason, they give surely to their employees for employment for a minimum fixed tenure of time.
**Which principle of management is followed here.**

A. Esprit de crops
B. Stability of tenure of personnel
C. Subordination of individual interest to general interest.
D. Fair remuneration to workers.

| 35. | ASSERTION(A): - Competitors, suppliers and customers directly affect the business than other environments.<br>REASON(R): - Other environment includes economic environment, social environment, political etc.<br>**Find the correct option: -**<br><br>A. Both A and R are true and Reason is the correct explanation of Assertion.<br>B. Both A and R are true and R is not the correct explanation of A.<br>C. A is true and R is false.<br>D. A is false and R is true. |
|---|---|
| 36. | There are 780 workers that actually works in the company. Superiors and Superintendents are also here to keep proper eye on them and on their work. They also pass their grievances to other level of management and then motivate them to work again with full efficiency and effectiveness to achieve goals.<br>**About Which level of management discussed in above lines that pass worker grievances and motivate them also.**<br><br>A. Operational level management<br>B. Non-managerial level<br>C. Middle level management<br>D. Top-Level management |
| 37. | ASSERTION(A): - Business environment is the totality of all external factors<br>REASON(R): - As business environment is a group of many outside forces. That's why its nature is totality.<br>**Find the correct option: -**<br><br>A. Both A and R are true and Reason is the correct explanation of Assertion.<br>B. Both A and R are true and R is not the correct explanation of A.<br>C. A is true and R is false.<br>D. A is false and R is true |
| 38. | Amitabh Bachchan, the legendary Bollywood actor is often seen in a television advertisement of Gujrat tourism. In this particular advertisement he encourages people to visit Gujrat and spend more time there by quoting line "KUCHH DIN |

TOH GUZARO GUJRAT MEIN". **Identify what being marketed by Mr. Amitabh Bachchan in above case.**

A. Price about product
B. Place
C. Product information
D. Promotion of product

39. MOMI TRADING CO. have just checked their grievances list and analyzed that their workers want to increase efficiency in work by improving some conditions. So as an objective company ask low level management and ensuring about proper ventilation, water, electricity and cleanliness etc.
**Tell which of following function of low-level management discussed above.**

A. Submitting workers grievances in time.
B. Ensure proper working conditions
C. Ensure proper supply of every raw material
D. Ensure the affect the environment.

40. ASSERTION(A): - In scientific management, a worker work under 8 specialists simultaneously
REASON(R): - Scientific management violates the principle of unity of command.
**Find the correct option: -**

A. Both A and R are true and Reason is the correct explanation of Assertion.
B. Both A and R are true and R is not the correct explanation of A.
C. A is true and R is false.
D. A is false and R is true.

41. After independence, Govt. of India saw that economy of country gone to decline and in very difficult situation. There was a need to cut off the country from economic difficulty and speeding up the growth. As a result, Govt announced various economic reforms in 1991 with new economic policy.
**Which was the main common reforms?**

A. Liberalization and privatization
B. Liberalization and globalization

|   |   |
|---|---|
|   | C. Privatization and globalization<br>D. Liberalization, Privatization and Globalization |
| 42. | We can say that management is both science as well as an art. As a _____, management provides necessary guidance to managers to achieve practical efficiency. With reference to _____, it is in the form of best work technique, helps managers to face every type of situations successfully.<br><br>A. Art, science<br>B. Science, art<br>C. Science, science<br>D. Art, art. |
| 43. | It can be observed that _____ have influenced the Indian business and industry in positive way. The challenge emerging out of these reforms have been faced. The Indian market has become customer oriented and customer friendly techniques are being used to have better relations with the customers.<br><br>A. Social reforms<br>B. Political reforms<br>C. Economic reforms<br>D. All the above. |
| 44. | In relation to _____, it is said that, "The question is not weather there should be decentralization, but decentralization to what degree."<br><br>A. Limitations of decentralization<br>B. Importance of decentralization<br>C. Importance of organization<br>D. Importance of delegation. |
| 45. | The process of organization is<br>1. Establishing reporting relations<br>2. Assigning duties<br>3. Identification and division of work.<br>4. Departmentalization<br>**Arrange in correct order**<br><br>A. (2), (3), (4), (1)<br>B. (3), (4), (2), (1) |

C. (3), (4), (1), (2)
D. (3), (2), (1), (3)

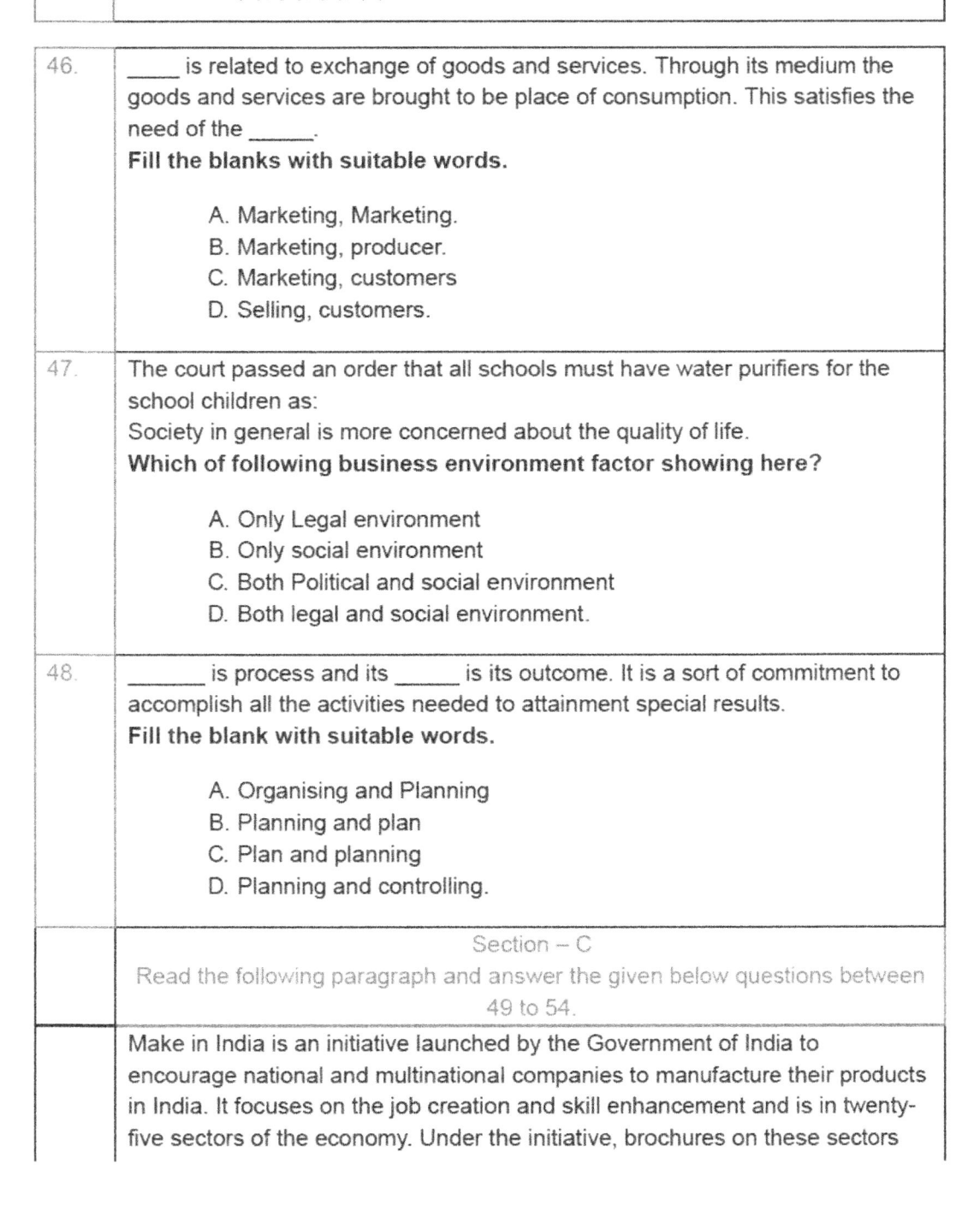

| 46. | _____ is related to exchange of goods and services. Through its medium the goods and services are brought to be place of consumption. This satisfies the need of the _____.<br>**Fill the blanks with suitable words.**<br><br>A. Marketing, Marketing.<br>B. Marketing, producer.<br>C. Marketing, customers<br>D. Selling, customers. |
|---|---|
| 47. | The court passed an order that all schools must have water purifiers for the school children as:<br>Society in general is more concerned about the quality of life.<br>**Which of following business environment factor showing here?**<br><br>A. Only Legal environment<br>B. Only social environment<br>C. Both Political and social environment<br>D. Both legal and social environment. |
| 48. | _____ is process and its _____ is its outcome. It is a sort of commitment to accomplish all the activities needed to attainment special results.<br>**Fill the blank with suitable words.**<br><br>A. Organising and Planning<br>B. Planning and plan<br>C. Plan and planning<br>D. Planning and controlling. |
|  | Section – C<br>Read the following paragraph and answer the given below questions between 49 to 54. |
|  | Make in India is an initiative launched by the Government of India to encourage national and multinational companies to manufacture their products in India. It focuses on the job creation and skill enhancement and is in twenty-five sectors of the economy. Under the initiative, brochures on these sectors |

| | | |
|---|---|---|
| | | and a web portal were released. The initiative aims at high quality standards and minimizing the impact on the environment. It also seeks to attract foreign capital investments in India. |
| | 49. | **Identify the dimensions discuss above?**<br><br>A. Economic environment<br>B. Economic environment, social environment and technology environment<br>C. Economic environment, political environment<br>D. Economic environment, political environment and technology environment. |
| | 50. | **Which of following lines quote that it is economic environment?**<br><br>A. Make in India is an initiative launched by the Government of India to encourage the national and multinational companies.<br>B. It also seeks to attracts the foreign capital.<br>C. Under this initiative, brochures on the twenty-five sectors and a web portal were released.<br>D. The initiative aims to high quality standards and minimizing the impact on environment. |
| | 51. | **Which value from below government wants to convey in above para?**<br><br>A. High quality standards<br>B. Concern for environment<br>C. Both a and b<br>D. Foreign capital enhancement. |
| | 52. | **Foreign capital is related to which of following environment?**<br><br>A. Economic environment<br>B. Social environment<br>C. Natural environment<br>D. Political environment. |
| | 53. | **Make in India is the concept come under?**<br><br>A. Management discipline.<br>B. Administration duties |

|  | C. Political environment concept |
|  | D. Factor of Business environment |

| 54. | **When Make in India started?** |
| --- | --- |
|  | A. 2015 |
|  | B. 2014 |
|  | C. 2016 |
|  | D. 2017 |

Answer the following questions from reading paragraph.
From 55 to 59

Aapna Vidyalaya' believes in the holistic development of students and encourages team building through a mix of curricular, co-curricular and sports activities. On its Founder's Day, a stage performance had to be put up. A committee of ten prefects was constituted to plan different aspects of the function. They all decided to use recycled paper for decoration. There was a spirit of unity and harmony and all the members supported each other. With mutual trust and a sense of belonging, the Programme was systematically planned and executed. Kartik, one of the prefects, realized that the group had unknowingly applied one of the principles of management while planning and executing the Programme. He was so inspired by the success of this function that he asked his father to apply the same principle in his business. His father replied that he was already using this principle.

| 55. | **Identify the principle of management applied for the success of the Programme.** |
| --- | --- |
|  | A. Stability of tenure or personnel |
|  | B. Esprit de crops |
|  | C. Authority and Responsibility |
|  | D. Unity of direction. |

| 56. | **Which feature of management from below options is highlighted above?** |
| --- | --- |
|  | A. Goal oriented |
|  | B. Dynamic |
|  | C. Group activity |
|  | D. Intangible force. |

| 57. | Which value show by "Apna Vidyalaya" communicated to society?<br><br>A. Responsibility<br>B. Environment control<br>C. Sustainable development<br>D. Both a and c |
|---|---|
| 58. | Which one more feature is highlighted in above para except 56 question.<br><br>A. Multi-dimensional<br>B. Flexible<br>C. Continuous process<br>D. Pervasive in nature. |
| 59. | How many principles does Henry Fayol give?<br><br>A. 10<br>B. 12<br>C. 14<br>D. 16 |
| 60 | A company need a detailed plan for its new project. "Construct of a shopping Mall."<br>**What type of plan it is?**<br><br>A. Policy<br>B. Procedure<br>C. Programme<br>D. Strategy |

## SAMPLE PAPER- 2 (CBSE)
### COMMERCE/BUSINESS STUDIES CLASS 12
### TERM 1 MODEL TEST PAPER

Minimum marks: 40

Time: - 90minutes.

### Section- A

Answer any 20 questions out of 24.

1. Which of following is not the correct statement?

    A. Management is a goal-oriented process.
    B. Management is a continuous process.
    C. Management is a dynamic process.
    D. Management is a rigid process.

2. Top-level management is concerned with

    A. Long term plans.
    B. Short term plans
    C. Guidelines for supervisors.
    D. None of these.

3. Principle of management are not

    A. Behavioral
    B. Absolute
    C. Universal
    D. Flexible

4. _____ is a technique in which each worker is supervised by eight supervisors.

    A. Functional foremanship
    B. Unity of action.
    C. Centralization
    D. Simplification of work.

5. Which is not the specific factor of business environment?

    A. Customers
    B. Suppliers
    C. Employees
    D. Technological conditions.

6. The growing awareness about healthcare has led to an increase in the demand for healthcare products and services in the country. Identify the feature of business

environment in above case?

    A. Dynamic
    B. Uncertainty
    C. Relativity
    D. Interrelatedness

7. Which of following is not the importance of planning?

    A. Reducing uncertainty.
    B. Identifying alternatives critically.
    C. Developing leadership.
    D. Selecting the most appropriate plan.

8. _____ are relevant to recurring activities.

    A. Single use plans.
    B. Standing plans.
    C. Objectives.
    D. Programmes.

9. It is defined as the framework within which managerial and operating tasks are performed.

    A. Span of management
    B. Organizational structure
    C. Informal Organization
    D. None of above

10. Rishabh has joined as a Creative Head in an entertainment company. He always ensures that the work has been divided into small and manageable activities and also the activities of similar nature are grouped together. **Identify the related step in organising process being mentioned above.**

    A. Identification and division of work.
    B. Departmentalization
    C. Assignment of duties.
    D. Establishing the reporting relationships.

11. Karan had decided to sell his range of organic food products through her own retail outlets.

**Identify the channel of distribution being adopted by the company.**

    A. Zero level channel
    B. One level channel
    C. Two level channels
    D. Three level channels.

12. Registering a trade mark gives users a

    A. Finance
    B. Fame
    C. Protection
    D. Information

13. Marketing is called a _____ process because it involves interaction of buyers and sellers.

    A. Social
    B. Legal
    C. Economic
    D. Political.

14. For heavy equipment, which of following channels is more relevant?

    A. Zero-level.
    B. One-level
    C. Two-level
    D. Three-level.

15. Which of following is not the demerit of the functional structure.

    A. It places more emphasis on the objectives pursued by functional head than an overall enterprise objective.
    B. It may lead to conflict of interest among departments due to varied interests.
    C. It leads to occupational specialization.
    D. It may lead to difficulty in coordination among functionally differentiated departments.

16. It arises from the established scalar chain which links the various job positions and levels of an organization.

    A. Authority
    B. Accountability
    C. Power
    D. Duty

17. Deepak is striving to earn a profit of 30%. in the current financial year.
**Identifying the type of plan being described in above lines.**

    A. Method.
    B. Objective
    C. Strategy
    D. Programme.

18. The last step of planning process is

        A. Plan implementation
        B. Follow up
        C. Alternative identification
        D. None of above.

19. Which of following is not a part of business environment?

    A. Customers
    B. Suppliers
    C. Competitors
    D. None of above.

20. On 8th November 2016, with the announcement from the government of India, all the 5000 and 1000 bank notes of the Mahatma Gandhi series have ceased to be a legal tender. The govt. also announced the issuance of new notes of 500 and Rs. 2000 banknotes.

**Identify the concept being described above.**

    A. Demonetization
    B. Liberalization
    C. Privatization
    D. Globalization

21. According to Henry Fayol, if the principle of general management is violated, "authority is undermined, discipline is in jeopardy, order distributed and stability threatened."

**Identify the principle.**

    A. Authority and responsibility
    B. Discipline
    C. Unity of command
    D. Equity

22. _____ means one plan and one boss.

    A. Unity of direction
    B. Unity of command
    C. Centralization
    D. Gang Plank.

23. The function of management that is related to right person at right place.

    A. Staffing
    B. Planning
    C. Controlling
    D. Directing.

24. Which is not the designation of related to middle level management?

A. Operating head
B. Sales manager
C. Chief executive officer
D. Divisional officer.

## Section – B

### Answer any 20 questions out of 25 to 48 questions.

25. Ashutosh Goenka was working in "Axe Ltd. a company manufacturing air purifiers. He found that the profits have started declining from the last six months. Profits has an implication for the survival of the firm, so he analyzed the business environment to find out the reasons for this decline.

**Identify the level of management at Ashutosh Goenka was working.**

A. Middle level
B. Top-level
C. Low-level
D. Non-managerial.

26. Mr. Nitin Singhania's father has a good business of iron and steel. He wants to go to the USA for his MBA but his father thinks that he should join the business. On the basis of emerging-trends, do you think that Mr. Singhania should send his son to the USA?

A. Yes
B. No
C. Don't say

27. ABC Ltd. is engaged in producing electricity from domestic garbage. There is almost equal division of work and responsibilities between workers and the management. The management even takes workers into confidence before taking important decisions. All the workers are satisfied as the behavior of the management is very good.

**State the principle of management describe above.**

A. Harmony not discords
B. Division of work
C. Corporate not individualism
D. Esprit de crops.

28. An automobile company is a leading manufacturing company in its segment. The company has decided to launch fully solar charged vehicles. This technology will cost the company Rs. 2000 crores annually. When he relationship manager of the company was asked about the reason of bearing so much extra cost he replied that the company considered environmentally friendly techniques as only the solution to increasing pollution. The company feels by bearing costs it is fulfilling its responsibility.

**Identify the marketing management philosophy?**

A. Product marketing
B. Production marketing
C. Societal marketing
D. Marketing philosophy.

29. A five-star hotel has decided to include picking up the clients from airports and railway stations. They will definitely improve the image of the hotel. It will add to the comfort of the clients. The hotel has done this to fight the tough competition with the new entrants in the market. This step is expected to increase the charges of the stay at the hotel.

**Identify the marketing mix in the above case?**

A. Product
B. Price
C. Place
D. Promotion.

30. In _____, with the view to earn more profit, priority is given to the consumer satisfaction.

**Fill up the blank with suitable word.**

A. Marketing
B. Selling
C. Production
D. Business

31. _____ is the medium of increasing the sales wherein both the buyer and seller directly face each other. The seller presents his product before the _____ describes its features and fully satisfies the probable buyer by removing all his doubts.

**Choose from given below, the correct one to fill up the blanks.**

A. Personal selling, buyer
B. Personal selling, product
C. Publicity, buyer
D. Publicity, seller.

32. Situation A: - Functional organization is formed on the basis of work.

Situation B: - Functional organization is helpful in specialization of job.

**Identify which statement is true?**

A. Both A and B are correct.
B. Both A and B are incorrect.
C. Statement A is correct and Statement B is incorrect.
D. Statement A is incorrect and Statement B is correct.

33. _____ cannot be delegated to some other person. It is only towards the _____.

Choose the correct words to fill ups.

   A. Authority, delegators.
   B. Accountability, responsibility
   C. Accountability and delegators.
   D. Accountability and authorities.

34. Read the following two and identify the organization structure from below options.

1. The expansion and growth are easier as the new units can be adjusted without disturbing the ongoing operations.

2. The training of managers is easier as the limited sets of skills are targeted for the particular employee.

   A. Divisional and divisional
   B. Functional and divisional
   C. Functional and Functional
   D. Divisional and functional.

35. Ajanta Foods Ltd. is engaged in the trading of "Noodles". It has its registered office in Kolkata, manufacturing unit in Solan and marketing department at Delhi.

**Which type of organizational structure the company should adopt to achieve its targets?**

   A. Divisional
   B. Informal
   C. Formal
   D. Functional

36. Rakesh calls his new subordinates for a meeting. He is a top-level manager. He arranges for a power point presentation to train his subordinates who are all middle level managers. He tells them the way of doing the task of treating suppliers through a new software system to be installed within 30 days.

**Identify the type of plan?**

   A. Strategy
   B. Procedure
   C. Method
   D. Programme.

37. Dheeraj is a very had working manager. After working for the implementation of his well chalked put plan, he from the start of July, decided to see in what ways and up to what accuracy has his plan been implemented.

**Which step the planning process will be involved by Dheeraj from starting of July?**

   A. Implementation of plan
   B. Follow up

C. Alternative identification
D. Setting objectives

38. If you fail to plan, you _____ to fail.

**Fill up the blank by correct word.**

A. Planning
B. Plan
C. Organize
D. Direct

39. Which of following is not the correct importance about planning?

A. Planning provides direction
B. Planning reducing overlapping and wasted activities.
C. Planning is futuristic.
D. Planning involves decision making.

40. Since a greater number of people have become more beauty and health conscious, our economy has witnessed an unprecedented surge in the number of health and beauty spas and wellness clinics. Related feature of business environment described in above lines: -

A. Totality of external forces
B. Dynamic nature
C. Interrelatedness
D. Relativity

41. In order to boost and double India's export of goods and services to over USD 1,000 billion by 2025. It is important to lower effective corporate tax rate, bring down cost of capital and simplify regulatory and tax framework.

**Identify the related dimension of business environment.**

A. Social and legal dimension.
B. Technology and political
C. Political and Social
D. Economic and legal dimension.

42. Under _____ system, business is directed and controlled by the government.

*Fill up with suitable word from below: -*

A. Capitalistic economy.
B. Socialistic economy
C. Mixed economy.
D. Both a and b

43. Statement 1: - Internal environment includes all those factors which influence business and which are present within the business itself.

Statement 2: - Internal factors are out of the control of business.

**Which of following is correct statement?**

    A. Both statement true
    B. Both statement false.
    C. Statement 1 is true and statement 2 is false.
    D. Statement 1 is false and statement 2 is true.

44. Mohan, a manager expects his subordinates to work for the happiness and pleasure of being in the organization.

**Which principle of management is being overlooked?**

    A. Order
    B. Unity of command
    C. Unity of direction.
    D. Scalar Chain.

45. Assertion(A): Coordination is the essence of management.

Reason(R): It is not a separate function of management, rather it forms major part of all other functions of management.

    A. Both A and R are true.
    B. Both A and R are true but R is not the correct explanation of A.
    C. A is true and R is false
    D. A is false and R is true.

46. The management cannot be treated as a _____, but as its principles are subject to change with time, situations and human nature, it is better to be called it _____.

**Fill ups by choosing correct option from below:**

    A. Applied science, perfect science.
    B. Perfect science and applied science.
    C. Both perfect science
    D. Inexact science and applied science.

47. In an organization employee are happy and satisfied, there is no chaos and the effect of management is noticeable.

**Which characteristic of management is highlighted by the statement?**

    A. Management is social process
    B. Management is intangible force.
    C. Management is group activity
    D. Management is discipline.

48. Statement A: Lower level management is also called operational level management.

Statement B: Operational level consists of all the departmental heads.

Which of above statement is correct?

A. Both A and B statement is correct.
B. Statement A is correct and B is incorrect.
C. Statement B is correct and Statement A is incorrect.
D. Both A and B are incorrect statements.

## Section- C

*Answer any 10 question from questions from 49 to 60.*

Read the following paragraph and answer the questions from 49 to 52.

Jayant is working as Head Relationship Manager in the wealth management division of a private sector bank. He has created an internal environment which is conducive to an effective and efficient performance of his team of ten relationship management executive" A typical day at work in Jay ant's life consists of a series of interrelated and continue functions. He decides the targets for his department which are in line with the objectives of the organization as a whole. The future course of action for his team members is laid out well in advance. The various resources required by the relationship managers like an iPad with GPS system, account opening forms, brochures, details of account holders etc. are made readily available to them. The executives are given sufficient authority to carry out the work assigned to them. Jayant works in close coordination with the Human Resource Manager in order to ensure that he is able to create and maintain a satisfactory and satisfied workforce in his department. Through constant guidance and motivation, Jayant inspires them to realize their full potential. He offers them various types of incentives from time to time keeping in view their diverse individual needs. Moreover, he keeps a close watch on their individual performances in order to ensure that they are in accordance with the standards set and takes corrective actions whenever needed.

49. Identify the concept being referred to in the following line, "He has created an internal environment which is conductive to an effective and efficient performance of his team of ten relationship management executives."

A. Planning
B. Organizing
C. Coordination
D. Management

50. Identify the one of the functions of the concept given in question no. 49?

A. Planning
B. Coordination
C. Management
D. Decentralization

51. The various resources required by the relationship managers like an iPad with GPS system, account opening forms, details of account holders etc. are made readily available

to them. The executives are given sufficient authority to carry out the work assigned to them.

Identify the concept discuss by above line from above paragraph?

- A. Planning
- B. Coordination
- C. Organising
- D. Directing.

52. Organising is the main function of management. After which function this function perform in management?

- A. Planning
- B. Staffing
- C. Directing
- D. Controlling.

Read the following paragraph and answer the questions from 53 to 55.

A company has been registered under the Companies Act with an authorized share capital of Rs.20,000 crores. Its registered office is situated in Delhi and manufacturing unit in a backward district of Rajasthan. Its marketing department is situated in Bhopal. The company is manufacturing Fast Moving Consumer Goods (FMCG).

53. Which organizational structure suitable for this company?

- A. Functional organization
- B. Divisional organization
- C. Centralization structure or business
- D. Decentralization structure of business.

54. Which is not an advantage of functional organization?

- A. Development of divisional heads.
- B. Benefits of specialization.
- C. Managerial efficiency increased.
- D. Equal weightage to all functions.

55. Divisional organization is specialized in the

- A. Job
- B. Product
- C. Work
- D. None of these.

Identify the marketing management philosophy involved in the following cases:

- A. Product Philosophy
- B. Production philosophy

C. Selling philosophy
D. Societal philosophy

56. Geetika scooters are the leading manufacturers of scooters in the industry. They have the first mover advantage in the industry. When they started manufacturing scooters no other company was doing it. They manufacture scooters and the middle class purchases them in a high number. With each passing year the number of scooters sold is increasing. The company's main concern usually is to produce maximum number of scooters. Company's profit is governed by the maximum number of scooters they produce.

57. Aman microwaves produce microwaves but they do not try to understand the needs of the customers. Their main focus is always on the quality of the product but never on customer requirement. They try' to include as many features as possible in their product. This year they have added a special type of alarm in their product which is a unique feature. The alarm is available in ten varieties. However, the customers say that the product is not of much use to them as it consumes a lot of electricity.

58. Ravi coolers is a very progressive company. The owners of the company feel that unless and until they contribute to society it is worthless to exist as a company. In a recent move by the government the organization has decided to help it. The organization will be making five teams of hired environmentalists from foreign countries. This team will help the local people clean the portions of a polluted river in the country. The costs of this project will be borne by the company.

59. A company decides to do promotion for a new chips flavor. For this many contest are organized in different colleges. The youth is the target market for the chip's makers. However, there hasn't been proper research about the liking of the flavor among the youth. The company has launched this product based only on intuition. The company has decided to go ahead with the promotional campaign even if there is a negative response from the buyers.

60. A company is manufacturing a new type of helicopter for the rich people. The helicopters manufactured are patented products of the company. No other company has made this type of helicopter yet. The company says since the helicopter is unique the booking of the product is done in advance by the buyers. There has been demand in excess. The company is in no need to market its product. It has to see that it can make the helicopter available to people who can buy it.

## SAMPLE PAPER- 1 (ISC/ICSE)
### COMMERCE CLASS 12
### TERM 1 MODEL TEST PAPER

MINIMUM MARKS: - 40

EACH QUESTION CARRU EQUAL MARKS.

1. An increase or decrease in value of rupee is an example of: -
    a) Economic environment
    b) Social environment
    c) Political environment
    d) None of these

2. Relaxation the restriction and controls imposed on business and industry means
    a) Liberalization
    b) Privatization
    c) Globalization
    d) None of these

3. Which of following does not explain the impact of government policy changes on business and industry?
    a) More demanding customers
    b) Increasing competition
    c) Market orientation
    d) Changes in agricultural prices

4. Short-term investment decisions also called?
    a) Working capital
    b) Dividend decisions
    c) Capital budgeting
    d) None of above

5. The cheapest source of finance is
    a) Retained earnings
    b) Debentures
    c) Equity share capital
    d) None of above

6. Higher working capital results in
    a) Higher equity, lower risk and lower profits.
    b) Higher current ratio, higher risk and higher profits
    c) Lower current ratio, lower risk and lower profits
    d) Lower equity, lower risk and higher profits.

7. Dividend is paid only on

a) Shares
b) Debentures
c) Borrowed capital
d) Loans

8. Which company firstly in India to issue convertible zero interest debentures in January 1990?

   a) Reliance Co.
   b) Adani Enterprise
   c) Tata Motors
   d) Mahindra and Mahindra

9. During week days, NEFT takes place

   a) 5 times a day
   b) 3 times a day
   c) 4 times a day
   d) 6 times a day

10. The work performed by top-level management is

    a) Concerned with control of operative employees.
    b) Complex and stressful.
    c) Easy
    d) Not considered

11. Pramod Limited targets production of 22000 units in a year. The production manager was able to cut down the cost but could achieve the target. In this case, manager is _____ but not_____.

    a) Efficient but not honest.
    b) Effective but not efficient
    c) Efficient but not effective
    d) None of above

12. Coordination is the

    a) Essence of management
    b) Function of management
    c) An objective of management
    d) None of above.

13. She/he keeps machine, materials, tools etc. ready for the operations to concerned about workers? Whose work is described by the sentence with functional foremanship?

a) Instruction card clerk
b) Route clerk
c) Gang boss
d) Repair boss

14. Unity of direction is related to
    a) One head and one plan.
    b) One head and different plans
    c) Planning by production manager
    d) Planning by employees

15. Principles of management cannot be
    a) Tested in laboratories
    b) Defined
    c) Applied science
    d) Part of business.

16. The first step of planning process is
    a) Setting the objective
    b) Selecting alternative
    c) Follow up action
    d) Implement the plan

17. Planning seeks to bridge the gap between
    a) Present and past position
    b) Past and present position
    c) Present and future position
    d) None of above.

18. Training, lectures and seminars are the part of
    a) Method
    b) Procedure
    c) Strategy
    d) Policy

19. Amisha is the director of the company. At which level does Amisha stands in management?
    a) Top-level
    b) Middle-level

c) Low-level
d) Non-managerial level

20. Sachin, a manager expects his subordinates to work for the happiness and pleasure of being in the organization. Which principle of management is being overlooked?
    a) Principle of initiative
    b) Principle of equity
    c) Remuneration to employees
    d) Principle of stability of tenure.

CHOOSE THE ODD ONE OUT: -

21. Micro environment consists of
    a) Top management structure
    b) Mission and objectives
    c) Corporate culture
    d) Public

22. Fixed capital means investment in
    a) Machinery
    b) Cash
    c) Furniture
    d) Plant

23. Long term source of finance are
    a) Debentures
    b) Public deposits
    c) Retained earnings
    d) Equity shares

24. Henry Fayol principles include
    a) Principle of order
    b) Principle of discipline
    c) Principle of harmony not discord
    d) Principle of Stability of tenure.

25. Management is defined as
    a) Goal-oriented process
    b) Social process
    c) Individual Process

d) Continuous process

TICK THE CORRECT SENTENCE: -

26. Which sentence is true about SWOT analysis?
    a) A Strength is an inherent capability of company which it can use to decline the competitors.
    b) A weakness is the inherent limitation of compony that results in low profits for the company.
    c) An opportunity is the favorable condition that strengthen the working conditions of the company.
    d) A threat is an unfavorable condition in company' external environment which causes a damage or risk to position.

27. Which sentence is true advantage of planning?
    a) Planning is not a time-consuming process.
    b) Planning is not an expensive process
    c) Planning facilities decision making.
    d) Planning bridges gap between past and future.

28. One of the right facts about management is
    a) Management is an individual activity since a manager is only manage all the work.
    b) Management is interpersonal activity because in order to get things from other, a manager have to interact with others.
    c) Management is science because it is most creative in nature.
    d) Management is an art because one has to use his ideas in decision making.

29. Investors have an advantage of preference shares because
    a) There is flexibility in issuing preference shares.
    b) In case of cumulative preference shares the arrears of dividend also accumulate and payable in future.
    c) Issue of these shares does not involve any charge.
    d) The cost of raising finance from these shares is low.

30. The role of financial planning is evident from
    a) Financial planning helps in effective utilization of resources.
    b) It gives business lot of surprises in future.
    c) A sound financial planning helps in to avoid use of funds.
    d) It helps in basis for capital structure to get benefit to company by minimum return to shareholders.

READ THE TEXT GIVEN BELOW AND ANSWER THE FOLLOWING QUESTIONS FROM 31 TO 33.

India's retail sector has been undergoing structural changes for the last two decades. On one hand, the 'mall culture' has gradually become a way of life, especially in the metros and minimetros. On the other hand, there is accelerated growth in e-business as customers also prefer to buy products and services via the Internet, telephone and television. However, operating in either of the segments is marked by the presence of strong competitors.

31. Identify the specific forces discussed in above paragraph?
    a) Customers and competitors
    b) Customers and suppliers
    c) Suppliers and Financiers
    d) Customer and public.

32. Identify the general forces discussed above?
    a) Economic and social
    b) Social and technological
    c) Technological and political
    d) Legal and social.

33. Which factors affect the business environment?
    a) Micro factors
    b) Macro factors
    c) Both a and b
    d) None of above

READ THE FOLLOPWING TEXT AND ANSWER THE GIVEN BELOW QUESTIONS FROM 33 TO 36.

Josh Ltd. is a one of the largest two-wheeler manufacturers in India. It has a market share of about 42% in the two-wheeler category. The company had witnessed almost a 35% drop in the booking as the currency crunch was prompting people to withhold new purchases due to demonetization. Therefore, the production manager of the company had decided to align production to factor in slower sales in the market.

34. Identify the function of management highlighted in above paragraph?
    a) Planning
    b) Organising
    c) Staffing

d) Controlling

35. Which of following limitation of planning is highlighted above?
    a) Planning may not work under dynamic environment.
    b) Planning is rigid in nature
    c) Planning reduce creativity
    d) Both a and b

36. Which main factor is highlighted above which results in limitation of planning?
    a) Currency issues
    b) Demonetization
    c) Lack of Ideas
    d) Huge decline in shares.

READ THE FOLLOWING TEXT AND ANSWER THE QUESTIONS GIVEN BELOW FROM 37 TO 40.

"A business that doesn't grow dies", says Mr. Shah, the owner of Shah Marble Ltd. with glorious 36 months of its grand success having a capital base of RS.80 crores. Within a short span of time, the company could generate cash flow which not only covered fixed cash payment obligations but also create sufficient buffer. The company is on the growth path and a new breed of consumers is eager to buy the Italian marble sold by Shah Marble Ltd. To meet the increasing demand, Mr. Shah decided to expand his business by acquiring a mine. This required an investment of RS.120 crores. To seek advice in this matter, he called his financial advisor Mr. Seth who advised him about the judicious mix of equity (40%) and Debt (60%). Mr. Seth also suggested him to take loan from a financial institution as the cost of raising funds from financial institutions is low. Though this will increase the financial risk but will also raise the return to equity shareholders. He also apprised him that issue of debt will not dilute the control of equity shareholders. At the same time, the interest on loan is a tax-deductible expense for computation of tax liability. After due deliberations with Mr. Seth, Mr. Shah decided to raise funds from a financial institution.

37. Identify and explain the concept of Financial Management as advised by Mr. Seth in the above situation.
    a) Capital structure
    b) Capital budgeting
    c) Fixed capital
    d) Working capital

38. The answer of part 1 is the composition of which sources of finance?
    a) Long term sources
    b) Short term sources

c) Medium term sources
d) All the above

39. Which of following factors from above paragraph affect the part (1) i.e. answer of question number 37.

   a) Risk consideration
   b) Control
   c) Need of investors
   d) Both a and b

40. When a company uses borrowed capital with equity the it is called?

   a) Financial leverage
   b) Fixed capital
   c) Capital budgeting
   d) Borrowed capital.

| 1. A | 2. A | 3. D | 4. A | 5. A |
|------|------|------|------|------|
| 6. B | 7. A | 8. D | 9. D | 10. B |
| 11. C | 12. A | 13. C | 14. A | 15. A |
| 16. A | 17. C | 18. A | 19. A | 20. C |
| 21. D | 22. B | 23. B | 24. C | 25. C |
| 26. D | 27. C | 28. B | 29. B | 30. A |
| 31. A | 32. B | 33. C | 34. A | 35. D |
| 36. B | 37. A | 38. A | 39. D | 40. A |

## SAMPLE PAPER- 2 (ISC/ICSE)
### COMMERCE CLASS 12
### TERM 1 MODEL TEST PAPER

MINIMUM MARKS: - 40

EACH QUESTION CARRU EQUAL MARKS.

1. Under which of following function of management, policy and strategies formulated?

   A. Coordination
   B. Directing
   C. Organising
   D. Planning.

2. Management as an activity means:

    A. A team managing organization.
    B. A series of interrelated functions performed in every organization.
    C. A specialized subject of study.
    D. Getting done through others.

3. If Sachin is the finance manager of the Department A then at which level does Sachin works?

    A. Top-level
    B. Middle-level
    C. Low-level
    D. All levels.

4. In which principle of management, gang plank followed?

    A. Order
    B. Scalar chain
    C. Unity of direction
    D. Unity of command.

5. Principle of management are not

    A. Flexible
    B. Absolute
    C. Behavioral
    D. Universal

6. It prevents overlapping of various activities.

    A. Unity of direction.
    B. Unity of command
    C. Scalar chain
    D. None of these

7. Which of following factor directly affect the business environment?

    A. Legal regulatory environment.
    B. Market intermediaries
    C. Social trends
    D. Economic reforms.

8. Example of general forces

    A. Customers
    B. Market intermediaries
    C. Legal acts.
    D. Competitors.

9. Reduction in taxes rate is the reform under

    A. Liberalization
    B. Privatization
    C. Globalization
    D. All of above.

10. Which of following is not the limitation of planning?

    A. Planning creates rigidity.
    B. Planning doesn't work in dynamic environment
    C. Planning reduces creativity.
    D. Planning reduces the overlapping of wasteful activities.

11. Statement A: - Planning proceeds other functions.

Statement B: - Planning is an intellectual process.

Choose the right statement from above two?

    A. Statement A is correct and B is incorrect.
    B. Statement B is correct and A is incorrect.
    C. Both A and B statement correct.
    D. Both A and B incorrect.

12. _____ has gained importance because of uncertain and constantly changing business environment.

Fill up the blank with suitable word.

    A. Organising
    B. Directing
    C. Coordination
    D. Planning.

13. The minimum amount in RTGS transaction is Rs.

    A. One lakh
    B. Two lakhs
    C. Three lakhs
    D. Five Lakhs

14. When the whole capital of company is divided into fractions, then it called

    A. Bonds
    B. Shares
    C. Preference shares
    D. All the above.

15. Which of following have low minimum value?

A. Preference shares
B. Debentures
C. Equity shares
D. Both a and b

16. When company having large undistributed profits issue fully paid-up shares to their existing Shareholders free of charge in proportion to their existing shareholdings, they are called_____.

A. Right shares
B. Equity shares
C. Sweat equity shares
D. Bonus shares.

17. Trade credit is the

A. Short term source of finance.
B. Medium term source of finance.
C. Long term source of finance
D. Both b and c

18. The capital invested in the fixed assets of the firm is called _____.

A. Fixed capital
B. Working capital
C. Issued capital
D. All of these.

19. Gross working capital = _____.

A. Current assets – current liabilities
B. Book value of all current assets.
C. Current liabilities
D. Net current assets – Gross current liabilities.

20. How scale of operations affects the fixed capital of firm?

A. Smaller the scale, larger the fixed capital
B. Smaller the scale, smaller the requirements of fixed capital
C. Larger the scale, larger the requirements of fixed capital.
D. Larger the scale, small need of fixed capital.

Choose the odd one:

21. Working capital consist of

A. Cash
B. Bill receivable
C. Debtors

D. Creditors

22. Business environment is the totality of

    A. Legal acts
    B. Economic reforms
    C. Corporate culture.
    D. Customers.

23. Taylor gives an idea to do the work by using various techniques like: -

    A. Simplification
    B. Mental revolution
    C. Time study
    D. Science not rules of thumb.

24. Management is an

    A. Intangible force
    B. Interactive activity
    C. Inclusion of group people
    D. Individual activity.

25. Examples of objectives are: -

    A. To cross the 20000 crores mark in turnover in this year.
    B. To reduce quality rejects to 3%.
    C. No employee starts work or return to work under influence of drugs.
    D. To improve the communication system to hold the regular staff meeting and publish newsletter.


Choose the correct sentence: -

26. Top-level management is the highest level in the organization that perform various functions like

    A. Determine the objectives for the organization.
    B. Ensuring the work performance by providing better working environment.
    C. Issuing the instructions to all the staff so that proper interpretation would be make in the organization.
    D. Creating the better relations in the organization.

27. Economic environment is the mixture of all the economic system, policies and conditions of the economy. It also includes the factors of

    A. Industrial dispute act
    B. Import export policy

C. Religious values and traditions.
D. Constitutional framework.

28. EFT is the electronic funds transfer which has an advantage of.

   A. Due dates not a part of EFT.
   B. Expenses are less in this case.
   C. Transactions are effortless.
   D. One to one special dealings.

29. Preference shares are those that gives more preference to shareholders more than equity but have disadvantage too regarding:

   A. Trading on equity possible.
   B. No charge on assets.
   C. Full flexibility.
   D. Little appeal to investors.

30. Working capital is very important part of the organization due to: -

   A. Payment of the fixed expenses
   B. Continuity in production.
   C. Purchasing of machinery.
   D. Success only depends on this capital.

Read the following paragraph and answer the questions from 31 to 33.

Wireworks Ltd. is aa company manufacturing different kinds of wires. Despite fierce competition in the industry, it has been able to maintain stability in its earning and as a policy, uses 30% of its investors are very happy with the company as it has been declaring high and stable dividend over past five years.

31. Why company is declaring high rate of dividend?

   A. Nature of business
   B. Stability of earnings
   C. Competition
   D. Satisfaction to investors.

32. Which line from the below quote that company have to choose the reason in (31).

   A. The small investors are very happy with company as been declaring high rate of dividend.
   B. Company has stable dividend over past five years.
   C. As a policy company uses 30% of its profits to distribute dividend.
   D. Despite fierce competition in the industry, it has been able to maintain stability of earnings.

33. Why do you think small investors become too happy with company?

A. For stable dividend
B. For more earnings
C. For 30% distribution of dividend.
D. For stable earnings of business.

Read the following paragraph and answer the questions from 34 to 37.

ABC Ltd. in engaged in producing electricity from domestic garbage. There is almost equal division of work and responsibilities between workers and management. The management even takes workers into confidence before taking important decisions. All the behavior of workers is satisfied as the behavior of the management is very good.

34. Which principle of management is highlighted in above paragraph?

   A. Harmony not discords.
   B. Cooperation not individualism
   C. Division of work
   D. Authority and responsibility.

35. The principle in above 34 question is the extension of

   A. Harmony not discords
   B. Cooperate not individualism
   C. Division of work
   D. Authority and responsibility

36. Which values from below company shows in above paragraph to communicate to society?

   A. Participation
   B. Trust
   C. Sharing
   D. Prosperity

37. Except values in 36 question one more value is showing in this line ABC Ltd. in engaged in producing electricity from domestic garbage, what will be this value?

   A. Environment protection
   B. Best use of garbage
   C. Sustainable development.
   D. All of above.

Read the following paragraph an answer the questions given below 38 to 40.

Yamini bought three hundred 10% preference shares of ABC Ltd. in the year of 2016. The face value of each share is Rs. 100. She didn't receive any dividend on them during 2016 due to insufficient profits. In the year 2017 the company made surplus profits. Calculate the amount payable to her in year 2017 assuming that she is holding Cumulative and Non-cumulative shares.

38. In year 2016 dividend due to Yamini is in case of cumulative preference shares.

    A. 2000
    B. 5000
    C. 4000
    D. 3000

39. In Year 2017, dividend due to Yamini s in case of cumulative Shares.

    A. 3000
    B. 4000
    C. 5000
    D. 4500

40. In case of Non-cumulative shares, the value of dividend due to Yamini in year of 2017?

    A. 3000
    B. 4000
    C. 5000
    D. 6000

| 1. d | 2. d | 3. b | 4. b | 5. b |
| 6. a | 7. b | 8. c | 9. a | 10. d |
| 11. c | 12. b | 13.b | 14. b | 15. c |
| 16. d | 17. a | 18. a | 19. b | 20. C |
| 21. d | 22. c | 23. d | 24. d | 25. c |
| 26. a | 27. b | 28. c | 29. d | 30. b |
| 31. b | 32. d | 33. a | 34. b | 35. a |
| 36. a | 37. c | 38. d | 39. a | 40. a |

# SAMPLE PAPER- 3 (ISC/ICSE)
## COMMERCE CLASS 12
## TERM 1 MODEL TEST PAPER

**MINIMUM MARKS: - 40**
**EACH QUESTION CARRU EQUAL MARKS.**

1. Development of new product is the
    a) Strategy
    b) Programme
    c) Procedure
    d) Policy

2. Plans made in view to competitors plans
    a) Strategy
    b) Procedure
    c) Programme
    d) Policy

3. Which is not the part of legal environment?
    a) Deregulation of capital market
    b) Foreign policy
    c) Income distribution
    d) Literacy standards

4. External environment trends are changes will provide
    a) Threats
    b) Goodwill
    c) Less competition
    d) Profits

5. Fayol concentrated on
    a) Operational management
    b) General management
    c) Technical management
    d) Financial management

6. The study through which the timing of rest as determined is called
    a) Time study

b) Motion study
   c) Fatigue study
   d) Method study

7. Which is not the function of management?
   a) Staffing
   b) Coordination
   c) Cooperating
   d) All of above.

8. Is management a profession?
   a) Yes
   b) No
   c) Developing as a profession
   d) None of above

9. Which of following study not concerned with FW Taylor?
   a) Motion study
   b) Scalar chain.
   c) Method study
   d) Fatigue study

10. The scope of power of authority of manager expands with upward movement
    a) In his salary
    b) In his length of service
    c) In the number of subordinates under his control
    d) In his position in management hierarchy.

11. Higher debt-equity ratio results in
    a) Higher degree of financial risk
    b) Higher degree of operating risk
    c) Higher EPS
    d) Lower financial risk.

12. Short term investment decisions affects
    a) Purchase of fixed assets
    b) Long term profitability
    c) Day-to-day working of the business

d) Large amount of funds for future.

13. The minimum value of RTGS is
    a) 2 LAKHS
    b) 1 LAKH
    c) 3 LAKHS
    d) 4 LAKHS

14. Which of following statement is True?

Statement 1: - NEFT transactions take place in batches.

Statement 2: - NEFT cannot used to received foreign remittances.
    a) Both statements are False
    b) Both statements are True.
    c) Statement 1 is True but Statement 2 is false.
    d) Statement 2 is True and Statement 1 is false.

15. Mrs. Amisha is a president of ICAI. Her husband Sachin is also a vice president of ICAI.

Tell, at which level Both husband and wife working?
    a) Mrs. AMISHA – TOP LEVEL AND MR. SACHIN – MIDDLE LEVEL
    b) BOTH AT TOP LEVEL MANAGEMENT
    c) BOTH AT MIDDLE LEVEL
    d) MR. SACHIN AT TOP LEVEL AND HER WIFE AT MIDDLE LEVEL.

16. Net working capital =
    a) Current assets
    b) Current liabilities
    c) Current assets – current liabilities
    d) Current assets + Current liabilities

17. Fixed capital is also known as
    a) Working capital
    b) Fixed asset capital
    c) Block capital
    d) Long-term capital

18. Which of following is the short-term finance
    a) Equity shares
    b) Debentures

c) Installment credit
   d) Retained earnings
19. Which of following shares bring cash to company's coffers?
   a) Bonus shares
   b) Right shares
   c) Free shares
   d) All the above
20. DO's and Don'ts are prescribed by?
   a) Strategy
   b) Rules
   c) Methods
   d) Procedures

CHOOSE THE ODD ONE

21. The functions of management are?
   a) Planning
   b) Staffing
   c) Controlling
   d) Coordination
22. Violation of principle of order
   a) Right man and right job
   b) Confusion and chaos
   c) Wastage of resources
   d) Increase in cost of operations
23. Management as an art defined as
   a) Practical knowledge
   b) Universal validity
   c) Perfection by practice
   d) Personal skills
24. The lot of factors affecting the fixed capital
   a) Seasonal variations
   b) Method of production
   c) Intangible assets
   d) Nature of business

25. In concept to SWOT analysis, the weakness of HUL Ltd.
    a) Unfavorable prices in oils.
    b) Dispersed manufacturing locations
    c) Low-priced competitions
    d) Change in fiscal benefits

TICK THE CORRECT SENTENCE: -

26. Some of the direct benefit of the business environment to any business is: -
    a) It monitors the relevant information regarding environment and helps business to make rules and objectives.
    b) It helps in aware the business credit wordiness.
    c) It helps the business to take first mover advantage
    d) It aware the customer to business product.

27. One of the main features of principle of management
    a) Principle of management is the general guidelines to business analysis.
    b) It is rigid in nature
    c) It based on the situations.
    d) It is absolute in nature.

28. Seasonal working capital opted for
    a) To meet extra contingencies in future
    b) To meet requirements during particular season.
    c) To meet special demands
    d) To meet contingencies at any time.

29. Which is the main advantage of equity shares to company?
    a) Equity shareholders enjoy voting rights.
    b) In boom period, the value of equity shares goes manifold.
    c) Company can raise any amount of capital with equity shares.
    d) The liability of equity shareholders is limited.

30. The main fact about RTGS is
    a) Only enabled CBS bank branches
    b) Fees charged to RTGS vary from bank to bank
    c) Both a and b
    d) The minimum transaction in RTGS is 3lakhs.

Read the following paragraphs and answer the questions from 31 to 35

Capital Budgeting means the decisions regarding investment in fixed assets that yields income for the long period. ABC Co. is the largest manufacturing company and required large amount of fixed capital to purchase fixed assets of the firm. It mainly includes the decisions regards to capital budgeting for the purpose to get advantages of long-term growth and more return due to high risk factor.

Company also turned to completed their day to day expenses with short term capital and hence always invests 20% of the profit towards it every year. Stable earnings and availability of raw material as well as seasonal growth are the major strengths of company by using this short-term capital over the past few years.

Company invests their earnings and make its structure with equity, preference and debentures as a long-term source. Company make its structure for the purpose to trading on equity i.e. fixed cost capital on basis on equity capital to increasing earnings to shareholders.

Answer the questions 31 to 35 on the basis of above paragraph?

31. What type of structure is making by the company?

    A. Financial structure
    B. Capital structure
    C. Structure of management.
    D. Long term funds structure.

32. What is the main benefit for company to make structure?

    A. Trading on equity
    B. Working capital
    C. Fixed capital
    D. Meet daily expenses

33. Which capital is useful in meeting day to day expenses for company?

    A. Fixed capital
    B. Working capital
    C. Capital of management
    D. Both a and b

34. What is trading on equity?

    A. Raising equity capital over debt.
    B. Raising the equity capital as well as debt capital.
    C. Raising the borrowed capital and preference share capital on basis of equity share capital.
    D. Raising the capital to earn over equity.

35. How much working capital is required by company in case of manufacturing business?

    A. Less than fixed capital
    B. More than fixed capital
    C. Just require more and more according to manufacturing need.
    D. Just required working capital according to seasons.

Read the following paragraph and answer the questions from 36 to 39.

A Purchase manager has to purchase 100 tons of raw material. His son happens to be supplier along with other suppliers in the market. The manager purchases the raw material from the firm of his son at a higher rate than market rate. This will profit the manager personally, but company suffers loss. This situation is undesirable.

36. This situation shows lack of which principle of management?

    A. Unity of direction.
    B. Unity of command
    C. Centralization.
    D. Subordination of individual interest to general interest.

37. Which interest lack with the company loss?

    A. Individual interest.
    B. General interest
    C. Both a and b
    D. None

38. What is the positive effect of the principle mentioned in ques. 36.

    A. Increase in jealousy.
    B. Hindrance in achieving goals
    C. It makes coordination among workers.
    D. Observing humanity.

39. The principle answered in ques. 36 is given by?

    A. Henry Fayol.
    B. F.W Taylor
    C. Peter Drucker.
    D. Kootnz' O Donnel

40. Which of following is related to one head and one plan?

    A. Unity of direction.
    B. Unity of command
    C. Unity of action.
    D. Scalar chain.

| 1. B | 2. A | 3. A | 4. A | 5. B |
| 6. C | 7. C | 8. C | 9. B | 10. D |
| 11. A | 12. C | 13. A | 14. B | 15. B |
| 16. C | 17. C | 18. C | 19. B | 20. B |
| 21. D | 22. A | 23. B | 24. A | 25. B |
| 26. C | 27. C | 28. B | 29. C | 30. C |
| 31. B | 32. A | 33. B | 34. C | 35. C |
| 36. D | 37. B | 38. D | 39. A | 40. A |

## SAMPLE PAPER- 1 (PSEB & Similar State boards)
### COMMERCE CLASS 12
### TERM 1 MODEL TEST PAPER

MINIMUM MARKS: - 40

EACH QUESTION CARRU EQUAL MARKS.

Instructions:

1. Question paper consists of two-parts Part A and B.
2. All questions are Multiple choice questions.

3. OMR sheet will provide to you for marking the answers. In case of any cutting or double circles no marks will give to you.

4. There is no negative marking. Each question carries equal mark.

Time: - 45 minutes.                                                                                           Marks: - 40

## PART – A

1. Which of following feature is considered management as an art?
    a) Service motive
    b) Based on experiments
    c) Universal application.
    d) Creativity

2. How the principles of management derived?
    a) On the basis of experiments
    b) On the basis of observations.
    c) On the basis of study.
    d) Both a and b

3. By removing the control on the capital market, a huge amount of capital was collected by issuing various new issues in primary market.

It is the impact showed by which of following dimension of the business environment?
    a) Social environment
    b) Economic environment
    c) Legal environment
    d) Political environment.

4. Which of the following is not the limitation of the planning?
    a) Planning creates rigidity.
    b) Planning does not work in dynamic environment
    c) Planning reduces creativity
    d) Planning reduces the overlapping of the wasteful activities.

5. The process of organising includes: -

(1) Departmentalization

(2) Assigning of duties

(3) Establishing the reporting relations.

(4) Identification and Division of work.

Choose the correct sequence of process.
    a) (1), (2), (4), (3)
    b) (4), (3), (2), (1)
    c) (4), (1), (2), (3)
    d) (4), (1), (3), (2)

6. If you are a first line manager, then you are at which level of management?
   a) Top-level management.
   b) Middle level management.
   c) Low-level management
   d) Non-managerial level

7. Match the following.

| 1) Discipline officer | (a) Check and compare each and every task with standards |
| 2) Route clerk | (b) keeping machines and tools ready for the use. |
| 3) Repair boss | (c) Keep check that all the work should done in disciplined manner. |
| 4) Inspector | (d) ensures the sequence of completing the particular task. |

   a) (4), (3), (1), (2).
   b) (3), (1), (2), (4)
   c) (3), (4), (1), (2)
   d) "(3), (4), (2), (1)

8. Which of following is not come under the economic environment?
   a) National income
   b) Industrial development
   c) Flow of capital
   d) Standard of living of people.

9. "The manager who acts without planning must learn to live without _____.
Choose the right word to fill the blank.
   a) Return
   b) Profit
   c) Initiative
   d) Success.

10. Which of following is related to occupational specialization?
    a) Functional structure
    b) Divisional structure
    c) Both a and b
    d) Centralization.

11. Bharat is running an ice cream parlor in a local market. Keeping in mind the changing perceptions about health among the people, one of his employee Abhiraj suggests to him

that they should introduce a range a flavored yogurt. Bharat accepts his suggestion as a result both the image and the profitability of his business increases.

Identify the dimension of business environment discuss above?

a) Economic
b) Social
c) Political
d) Legal

12. When the country's economy is integrated with the economy of rest of world, then this is called_____.

a) Privatization.
b) Globalization.
c) Liberalization.
d) None of above.

13. After developing premises, the next step to complete the planning process is____.

a) Evaluating the alternative course.
b) Identification alternative course of action.
c) Setting the objectives.
d) Selecting an alternative.

14. Which is not the advantage of the formal organization?

a) Stability of organization.
b) Easy to fix responsibility
c) No overlapping of works.
d) Fulfils social needs.

15. _____ is the orderly arrangement of group efforts to people unity of action in pursuit a common objective."

Fill up the blank with suitable word from options.

a) Management
b) Coordination
c) Planning
d) Cooperation.

16. Taylor's principles are applied

a) Universally
b) Special situations
c) Every situation
d) Only in case of production.

17. "No smoking in the factory" is the example of

a) Method
b) Objective
c) Policy

d) Rule.

18. Which of following is the essence of responsibility?
    a) Assigned the jobs.
    b) Obey the duties.
    c) To get decisions implemented
    d) Delegated the authority.

19. Archana is a dynamic CEO. In her organization she allows for autonomy and opportunity to perform multiple functions. This led to managerial development in her employees.

Which of following organizational structure discussed in above lines?
    a) Divisional
    b) Functional
    c) Decentralization
    d) Informal

20. Match the following: -

| 1) Method | (a) Guidance the employees while decisions |
| 2) Policy | (b) Determine the sequence to do work. |
| 3) Procedure | (c) Discuss about what, when, how to achieve specified goals. |
| 4) Programme | (d) Determine how different activities of procedure to be completed. |

   a) (2), (4), (3), (1)
   b) (2), (3), (4), (1)
   c) (2), (1), (4), (3)
   d) (2), (3), (1), (4)

21. ___ principle of management tells that manager should treat their subordinates in a just and kind manner so that they develop a feeling of dedication and attachment for their work.

Choose the correct one to fill-up.
    a) Initiative
    b) Esprit de crops
    c) Equity
    d) Discipline.

22. The management cannot treat as _____ science, but as its principles are subject to change with the time o it better to be called as _____ science.

Fill-up with suitable words from below.
    a) Applied science and perfect science

b) Inexact science and pure science
c) Perfect science and applied science
d) Perfect science and soft science.

23. Management is an
    a) Activity
    b) Process
    c) Tradition
    d) All of above.

24. Statement A: Taylor principles are related to the factory area.

Statement B: Fayol Principles are related to lower level of management.
   a) Both A and B statements are correct.
   b) Both A and B are incorrect statements.
   c) Statement A is correct and B is incorrect.
   d) Statement A is incorrect and B is Correct.

25. Josh is the one of the largest two-wheeler manufacturers in India. It has a market share about 42% in the two-wheeler category. The company had witnessed almost a 35% drop in booking as a currency crunch was promoting people to withhold new purchases due to demonetization. Therefore, the production manager of the company has decided to align production to factor in slower sales in the market.

Identify the concept discuss above?
   a) Planning
   b) Management
   c) Organizing
   d) Coordination

26. Which organization is based on the rules and regulations?
   a) Functional organization
   b) Divisional Organization
   c) Informal organization
   d) Formal organization

27. If we delegate the authority, we multiply it by _____; If we decentralize it, we multiply it by____.

Fill-up with the suitable words.
   a) Two, many
   b) Many and two
   c) Three and many
   d) Many and many.

28. In POSDCORB, R stands for,
   a) Responsibility
   b) Review

c) Reporting
d) Recheck

29. Ram father is working in the Reliance Co. and lead the various functional managers. Discuss its position in the management levels?

a) Top-level
b) Middle-level
c) Operational-level
d) Non-managerial level.

30. Which of the following is not the work study?

a) Motion study
b) Method study
c) Time study
d) Mental revolution.

## Part-B

31. If a retailer gives rebate to the customer, then he uses a method of

a) Publicity
b) Sales promotion
c) Advertising
d) Personal selling

32. Branding, packaging and labelling are the parts of

a) Price mix
b) Place mix
c) Promotion mix
d) Production mix

33. Under which philosophy, efforts are made to bring the cost of production minimum?

a) Production
b) Product
c) Marketing
d) Selling

34. Selling goods by producer to consumer with the help of retailers and wholesalers involves?

a) One-channel
b) Zero-channel
c) Three-level
d) Two-level.

35. A five start hotel has decided to include picking up of clients from airports and railway stations. They definitely improve the image of the hotel. The hotel has done the comfort of the clients. The hotel has done this to fight the tough competitions with the new entrants in the market.

Identify the marketing mix?

a) Product
b) Price
c) Place
d) Promotion

36. A TV manufacturing company is spending substantial amount of money to persuade the target customers to buy its TV sets through advertisements, personal selling and sales promotion techniques.

Identify the element of marketing mix in above case?

a) Place
b) Product
c) Promotion
d) Price

37. Which of the following philosophy of marketing has main objective to consumer welfare.

a) Marketing
b) Production
c) Selling
d) Societal

38. _____ refers to the aggregate of policies formulated with the view to successfully completing different marketing activities.

Fill the blank by choosing suitable word.

a) Place mix
b) Product mix
c) Marketing
d) Marketing mix

39. If a editor of a newspaper himself publishes information about the product or company, it is called as _____

a) Personal selling.
b) Publicity
c) Sales promotion
d) Advertising

40. Match the following.

| (1) Product concept | (a) Consumer satisfaction |
| (2) Production concept | (b) Attracting customers |
| (3) Selling concept | © Quantity of product |
| (4) Marketing concept | (D) Quality of product |

a) (4), (2), (3), (1)
b) (4), (3), (1), (2)
c) (3), (2), (1), (4)
d) (4), (3), (2), (1)

## SAMPLE PAPER- 2 (PSEB & Similar State boards)
### COMMERCE CLASS 12
### TERM 1 MODEL TEST PAPER

MINIMUM MARKS: - 40
EACH QUESTION CARRU EQUAL MARKS.

Instructions:

1. Question paper consists of two-parts Part A and B.

2. All questions are Multiple choice questions.

3. OMR sheet will provide to you for marking the answers. In case of any cutting or double circles no marks will give to you.

4. There is no negative marking. Each question carries equal mark.

Time: - 45 minutes.                                              Marks: - 40

# PART - A

1. Policy formulation is the function of

    (a) Top level Managers

    (b) Middle level Managers

    (c) Operational Management

    (d) None of the above

2. _____ provides a rational approach for setting objectives and developing appropriate courses of action for achieving predetermined objectives.

    (a) Directing

(b) Staffing
(c) Planning
(d) Controlling

3. "Grouping similar nature jobs into larger units called departments" is the step in the process of one of the functions of management. Identify the function of management. (a) Planning
   (b) Organising
   (c) Directing
   (d) Staffing

4. Taylor believed that there was only one best method to maximize efficiency. This method can be developed through study and analysis. Identify the principle of Scientific management being discussed above:
   (a) Harmony not discords
   (b) Science not rules of thumb
   (c) Development of each and every person to his or her greatest efficiency and prosperity
   (d) Cooperation not individualism

5. The Statement "Planning is a primary function", suggests that
   (a) Planning precedes other functions
   (b) Planning requires logical and systematic thinking
   (c) Plan is framed, it is implemented, and is followed by another plan, and so on
   (d) Planning is required at all levels of management as well as in all departments of the organisation.

6. Arrange the following steps in the process of organising in the correct sequence:
   (a) Assignment of duties
   (b) Departmentalization
   (c) Identification and division of work
   (d) Establishing reporting relationship

Choose the correct option:
 (a) (a); (b); (d); (c) (b)
 (c); (b); (a); (d)
 (c) (c); (b); (d); (a)
 (d) (b); (c); (a); (d)

7. Match the functional foreman in Column I, with their functions in Column II, and choose the correct alternative:

| Column-I | Column-II |
|---|---|
| A-Speed Boss | i) Keeps machine and tools ready for work |
| B-Gang Boss | ii) Proper working conditions of machin and tools |
| C-Repair Boss | iii) Checks quality of work |
| D-inspector | iv) Timely completion of work |

a) A - ii), B-iv), C-i), D - iii)

b) A - iv), B-i), c- ii), D - iii)

c) A-ii), B- iii), C-i), D - iv)

d) A-iv), B- iii), C - ii), D - i)

8. Which of the following is a benefit of planning?
 (a) Helps in avoiding confusion and misunderstanding.
 (b) Ensures clarity in thought and action.
 (c) Useless and redundant activities are minimized or eliminated.
 (d) All of the above.

9. Which one of the following sequences of process of management is correct?
 (a) Planning, Directing, Controlling, Organising, Staffing
 (b) Directing, Staffing, Planning, Organising, Controlling
 (c) Planning, Organising, Staffing, Directing, Controlling
 (d) Organising, Planning, Staffing, Controlling, Directing

10. Successful management ensures that:
    (a) Goals are achieved with least cost
    (b) Timely achievement of goals
    (c) Both of the above
    (d) None of the above

11. Identify the features of management as a profession
    (a) systematic body of knowledge
    (b) restricted entry
    (c) service motive
    (d) All of the above

12. The Statement "Planning is a primary function", suggests that
    (a) Planning precedes other functions
    (b) Planning requires logical and systematic thinking
    (c) Plan is framed, it is implemented, and is followed by another plan, and so on
    (d) (d) Planning is required at all levels of management as well as in all departments of the organisation.

13. Instability of tenure of persons in an organization is harmful for_____
    (a) Employees
    (b) Organisation
    (c) Both (a) & (b)
    (d) None of the above

14. "The nature of the relationship of our country with foreign countries", is a major element of
    which of the following components of the Business Environment?
    (a) Social Environment
    (b) Legal Environment

(c) Political Environment

(d) Economic Environment

15. Which of the following statements is not true with reference to planning?
    (a) Planning is a pre-requisite for controlling.
    (b) Planning does not lead to rigidity.
    (c) Planning enables a manager to look ahead and anticipate changes.
    (d) Planning facilitates co-ordination among departments and individuals in the organisation.

16. A manager, by delegation:
    (a) Cannot shift his authority to the subordinate
    (b) Cannot shift his responsibility to the subordinate
    (c) Can Shift both the above
    (d) None of these

17. It is not always true that just because a plan has worked before it will work again.
    Identify the related limitation of planning.
    (a) Planning leads to rigidity.
    (b) Planning reduces creativity.
    (c) Planning may not work in a dynamic environment.
    (d) Planning does not guarantee success.

18. The principle of management given by Fayol which aims at preventing overlapping of activities is:
    (a) Division of work
    (b) Unity of Command
    (c) Unity of Direction
    (d) Order

19. Which of the following was not the feature of New Economic Policy of 1991?

(a) Liberalisation
(b) Privatisation
(c) Globalisation
(d) Specialisation

20. _____ ensures that the subordinate performs tasks on behalf of the manager thereby reducing his workload and providing him with more time to concentrate on important matters.

(a) Decentralization
(b) Delegation of authority
(c) Authority
(d) Accountability

21. Name the concept that refers to the number of subordinates that can be effectively managed by a superior and determines the number of levels of management in the organisation.
(a) Organization structure    (b) Span of management
(c) Hierarchy of authority
(d) Delegation of Authority

22. Star Limited is a company dealing in metal products. The work is mainly divided into functions including production, purchase, marketing, accounts and personnel. Identify the type of organizational structure followed by the organization.
(a) Functional structure
(b) Relational structure
(c) Divisional structure
(d) None of the above

23. Which of the following quality a manager must possess to succeed in planning?

(a) Reflective Thinking
(b) Imagination

(c) Farsightedness
(d) All of these

24. Which step in the process of planning will precede the step in which the manager is required to make certain assumptions about the future, which are the base material upon which the plans are drawn.
(a) Implementing the plan
(b) Identifying alternative courses of action
(c) Setting objectives
(d) Selecting an alternative.

25. Name the process which co-ordinates human efforts, assembles resources and integrates both into a unified whole to be utilized for achieving specified objectives, (a) Management
(b) Planning
(c) Organising
(d) Directing

26. The denominations that were taken out of circulation after demonetization in 2016 were:
(a) 100, 500 and 1000
(b) 500 and 1000
(c) Only 1000
(d) 100 and 500

27. According to the technique of Scientific management "Differential Piece Wage system" How much more will a worker making 60 units earn as compared to a worker making 49 units? If the standard output per day is 50 units and those who make standard output or more than standard get Rs. 75 per unit and those below get Rs. 65 per unit.
(a) Rs. 4500
(b) Rs. 3185

(c) Rs. 1315 (d) Rs. 3250

28. Centralization refers to:
    (a) Retention of decision-making authority
    (b) Dispersal of decision-making authority
    (c) Creating divisions as profit centers
    (d) Opening new centers or branches

29. The salesman of ABC ltd. could not achieve his sales target of 1000 units, on enquiry it was found that he was not allowed to take decision related to give discount or credit to any of his customer. State the principle of Management violated in this case.
    (a) Principle of Division of work
    (b) Principle of authority and responsibility
    (c) Principle of order
    (d) None of these

30. Which of the following is an example of social environment?
    (a) Money supply in the economy
    (b) Consumer Protection Act
    (c) The Constitution of the country
    (d) Composition of family

PART – B

31. Which of the following statements is not true with regard to the concept of product?
    (a) It is a bundle of utility.
    (b) It is a source of satisfaction.
    (c) It is confined to physical product.
    (d) Both (a) and (b).

32. Marketing mix is the set of _____ that the firm uses to pursue its marketing objectives in the target market.
    (a) Production tools
    (b) Promotional tools
    (c) Marketing tools
    (d) Selling tools

33. _____ involves a variety of programs designed to promote and protect a company's image and its individual products in the eyes of the public.
    (a) Advertising
    (b) Personal selling
    (c) Publicity
    (d) Public relations

34. Which of the following statements is incorrect?
    (a) Marketing is a social process
    (b) Focus of the marketing activities is on customer needs (c) Marketing is merely a post-production activity.
    (d) Marketing mix is a wider term than product mix.

35. Which one of the following is not a marketing mix?
    (a) Product
    (b) Physical distribution
    (c) Product pricing
    (d) Production process

36. Marketing is called a____process because it involves interaction of buyers and sellers.
    (a) Economic
    (b) Social
    (c) Legal
    (d) Political

37. Match the Statement in Column I, with the Marketing concept in Column II, and choose the correct alternative:

| Statement | Marketing concept |
|---|---|
| 1. Scale of production | a) Product concept |
| 2. Quality of product | b) Selling concept |
| 3. Promotional activities | c) production concept |
| 4. Customer satisfaction | d) Marketing concept. |

(a) 1-a, 2-b, 3-d, 4-c
(b) 1-a, 2-c, 3-d, 4-b
(c) 1-c, 2-a, 3-b, 4-d
(d) 1-c, 2-a, 3-d, 4-b

38. Rita is a small entrepreneur involved in the manufacturing of hair wax. She finds that cost of production of 100 gm of hair wax is Rs. 250. He has decided to keep a margin of 15% as profit. Moreover, he has assessed that there is a free competition in this product segment. In the context of above case:
Identify the function of marketing being performed by Rita-

(a) Pricing
(b) Branding
(c) Labelling
(d) Promotion.

39. The meeting place of both buyer and seller for exchange of goods and service is termed as
(a) Business Organization
(b) Factory
(c) Market
(d) All of the above

40. The process of transfer of goods from one place to another i.e., from the place of manufacturing to the market where exchange of these is taken place:
(a) Distribution

(b) Segmentation
(c) Transportation
(d) Order Processing

Printed in Great Britain
by Amazon